YOUR
POODLE
PUPPY

by

Ernest H. Hart

illustrated by the author

Published by T.F.H. Publications, Inc., T.F.H. Building, 245 Cornelison Avenue, Jersey City, N. J. 07302. Distributed in the British Empire by T.F.H. Publications (London) Ltd., 13 Nutley Lane, Reigate, Surrey, England. In Canada by Clarke, Irwin & Company Ltd., Clarwin House, 791 St. Clair Avenue West, Toronto 10, Ontario, Canada. Printed in the U.S.A. by the lithograph process by T.F.H. Lithograph Corp., Jersey City, N. J. 07302.

Distributed to the Book Trade in the U.S.A. by Crown Publishers, Inc., 419 Park Avenue South, New York, N. Y. 10016.

contents

your poodle puppy

To my Aunt Blanche:

    Thanks for your sincere interest in everything that concerned
me and mine throughout the years.

cover painting by E. H. Hart.
photographs by Frasie Studio, Evelyn M. Shafer, Tauskey, George Pickow (Three Lions, Inc.), Louise Van Der Meid, Bill Francis, United Press, William P. Gilbert.

The most popular breed of the moment and well deserving his exalted place in the canine social strata, His Majesty, the Poodle.

chapter 1

THE POODLE PUPPY BEFORE BIRTH

The mystery of mammalian birth is an intriguing part of the complete dog breeding concept. One moment there is nothing but an impossibly obese bitch in a whelping box, apprehensively aware of the stirring of new life within, and attended by an anxious owner. The next moment, with the onslaught of labor pains and peristaltic movement, there are two animals in the whelping box, mother and canine child. The phenomenon of nativity has taken place and will continue at regular intervals, you hope, until genesis is complete and a fine and healthy litter of pups feed greedily at nature's milk bar.

But long before the puppies come into wriggling being they must be fed well to insure absolute and maximum health and vitality when they materialize from the mother's warm, protective womb into the harsh reality of life. The vehicle through which we accomplish this purpose is, of course, the mother bitch. She must be fed well for her own maintenance and for the normal development of the young in utero, particularly during the last thirty days of the gestation period.

The bitch must be in good health when she is bred. If she is not nature will generally take a hand and delay the coming of the heat period. She should be mature, not bred at her first heat, and a sound, healthy, typical specimen of the breed. A sample of her stool should have been brought to your veterinarian for a fecal examination shortly before her mating cycle began and, if there was any evidence of internal parasites, she should have been wormed, with a repeat dosage to follow within a week or ten days to eradicate any worms that may have hatched from worm eggs that were not eliminated. The bitch should not be wormed any later than a week after she has been bred. Any drug that can kill internal worms can possibly also harm the tiny, forming embryos within the pregnant female.

The mother-to-be should have had sufficient exercise so that she will not lose her muscular "tone" and overall strength and vitality. And, of the utmost importance, she must have been fed well and intelligently. By intelligently I mean that she should not be stuffed with supplements, the means some frantic breeders use in an effort to insure the whelping of healthy pups. Feed the bitch the same healthful,

Rothara's Merrymorn Nell Rose, a lovely Miniature bitch, here taking the non-sporting group under Charles A. Swartz at the Langley Kennel Club, 1958. Owned by Moss Oaks Kennels and handled by Anne Rogers.

The judge, Douglas Sheppard, is here shown putting up the group winner, Ch. Charm Maison's J.D. Replica, owned by Mrs. Nelle Austin, handled by Wendell Sammet.

well-balanced diet you have been giving her and feed her enough, but don't stuff her until she becomes fat. A fat bitch is never an easy whelper. A vitamin and mineral supplement should be incorporated into the food but used moderately. Many breeders philosophize that if a little bit is beneficial a lot will be that much more advantageous. The result of such irrational thinking is a heavy-handed application of supplements in the feeding pan to the detriment of the healthy, nourishing and extremely necessary bulk food of the regular balanced diet.

Every bit of food you give the bitch is nutritionally aiding in the fetal development within her. She must be provided with enough milk to produce calcium, meat for phosphorus and iron, and all the other essential vitamins and minerals in her high protein diet. By incorporating fresh liver in her food two or three times a week a month

Bitches in all of the three recognized sizes must be
well bred and fed to become good producers. On
the facing page is the Standard, Carillon Fiddle
De Dee, owned by Blanche Carlquist and handled
here to winners bitch by Anne Rogers under judge
Forest N. Hall. The bottom photo shows the
Miniature, Calvinelle Pristine of Kent, owned and
handled by Mrs. Calvin B. Hartman, Jr., winning
under Col. Edward McQuown. Above, on this page
is the Toy, Karja's Fairytale In Jet, owned by Mr.
Karl Rudzik, and handled to a nice win by Jane
Kamp under judge Reginald Sparkes.

before she is due to whelp, you will keep her from being constipated and aid in the coming, necessary production of milk for the litter. As the embryos develop the bitch's appetite will increase to keep up with the demands made upon her by the growing whelps. In the last two weeks of her pregnancy it is desirable to provide her with a hearty breakfast as well as her usual dinner, and a drink of milk between meals will also help feed the hungry, soon-to-be-born babies.

The puppies develop in the horns of the uterus, not in the "tubes" (Fallopian tubes), as is commonly thought. As they develop, the uteri horns lengthen and the walls expand to accommodate the rapid growth of the embryos. This embryonic growth of the puppies is a process of division of cells to form additional new cells and at each cell division of the fertilized female eggs each of the chromosomes also divide. These chromosomes are the gene packages, the inherited characteristics that have been supplied to the puppy by his sire and dam. When the myriad divisions of cells and chromosomes have reached completion the form-ing of living entities is accomplished and birth becomes a fact. Then, in the whelping box, we see before us living, squealing, Poodle puppies.

Death at birth and unthrifty puppies that either die or fail to mature into strong, healthy animals is due to several causes. Infection in any area of the female's reproductive system is one of the main causes of puppy deaths, before or after birth. Close inbreeding can cause a genetic linkage of lethal or semi-lethal faults that have been dormant in the germplasm for generations only to become obvious by affecting the embryonic puppies. Improper feeding or lack of sufficient and nutritious food is another factor that will cause puppies to be born dead or weak. Late, pernicious dosing for worms can bring harm to the unborn whelps, and breeding the bitch too often without a rest (particularly if her environment is not all it should be) can also bring disaster in its wake. Eclampsia, sometimes called "milk fever," is a metabolic disturbance prevalent in pregnant bitches whose diets lack in calcium and phosphorus. If she had been getting a good, balanced diet and plenty of milk, this condition is avoided. Mastitis, an udder infection, is a common cause of puppy deaths. It is generally mistaken by the uninformed for "acid milk," a condition which does not exist in dogs because the bitch's milk is naturally acid. The infection cuts off part of the milk supply and the whelps either die of infection or from starvation due to the lack of sufficient milk.

When labor begins pressure from within forces the puppies, one by one, toward the pelvis. Make sure that you have removed all long hair from around the udders to make them easily accessible to the pups when they arrive. Wash the udders in warm water and a bland soap, then rinse all soap off thoroughly and dry so that they will be clean for the

REPRODUCTIVE SYSTEM OF THE BITCH
1. Vulva 2. Anus 3. Rectum 4. Uterus 5. Kidney
6. Ovary 7. Ribs 8. Developing embryo 9. Vagina

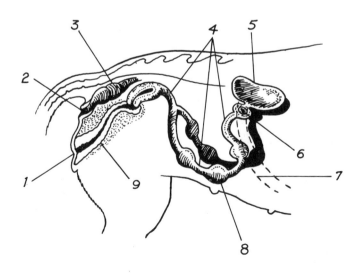

Standard, Bridget of Belle Glen, owned by Isabelle
McMullen, handled by Anne Rogers, going to
winners bitch under judge William Schmick.

coming nursing. The whelping box should have been made
familiar to the bitch at least a week before she was due to
whelp. A piece of oilcloth or rubber sheeting can be used as
a base flooring for the whelping box as it is easy to wash
and clean. On top of this can be laid newspaper, which
will be removed after the whelping is completed. The main
bedding for the bitch and her pups should be either straw,
hay, cloth, or torn up paper. Hay makes excellent bedding,
especially for Standards, because it retains its fresh smell
and imparts the pleasant odor to dam and puppies. The size
of the whelping box should be roughly 4 feet by 4 feet for
a dog the size of a very large Standard Poodle. These
dimensions should be shrunken according to the size of the
Poodle bitch. A medium Standard need not have a whelping
box larger than $3\frac{1}{2}$ foot square, and a Miniature which is up
to size can do very well in a $2\frac{1}{2}$ foot to 3 foot whelping box.

Toy bitches need about a 2 foot square whelping box.

Each puppy is born in a fetal envelope called the amoniotic sac which the bitch will tear open. If she waits too long to do this then the human attendant must break the sac open around the pup's face so it will not suffocate. Often the sac will rupture during birth and the puppy will be born leaving the sac still within its mother. The navel cord is connected through the sac to the placenta which generally accompanies the puppy at birth. If it is retained and the bitch chews off the cord that attaches it to the puppy (a completely normal and necessary act), the female will normally discharge from her uterus the lining to which the placentae were attached along with the placentae through which, during pregnancy, the young were fed.

Some bitches whelp rapidly, others don't. But, if several hours pass between the whelping of one puppy and the next it is best to call your veterinarian for expert advice. Don't worry if the pups are born head first or feet first; either way is normal.

Since this is a book about puppies and not about bitches and their breeding and whelping, I will delve no further into these aspects. The important thing to remember is that whatever you do, or whatever happens to the bitch, from the moment she is bred and the embryonic life within her caused by the breeding begins to form, also affects the puppies that will eventually be the end result of that breeding. So bring her to the mating in good physical shape, not exhausted from constantly producing puppies at every heat; feed her well with a nourishing, balanced diet during pregnancy; give her adequate exercise and supply her with a happy and familiar environment. Then, if all goes well, you will have a fine litter of healthy pups from your bitch which should be a credit to both your breeding acumen and your knowledge of animal husbandry. And, another and important consideration, you will show a nice profit from the sale of the pups to happy and satisfied customers.

chapter 2

THE POODLE PUPPY BORN

The time of waiting is past. We have planned the breeding carefully, selected the right stud dog and anxiously awaited with great expectations (apologies to Dickens) through approximately 60 trying days and nights for the blessed event which has at last taken place.

Now, though the puppies are being born and the whelping is proceeding with nice regularity, you cannot yet relax. As each pup is born and after the mother has been given ample time to lick and clean and fuss with the tiny whelp, you must put it on the mother's udders, first squeezing a little milk to the surface from the chosen nipple. Then, by holding the puppy's head and forcing its mouth against the warm teat you will spark instinct in the little creature and it will begin to suck and push with its front feet against the mother's breast.

All young that are obviously not normal should be culled

Suzettes Petite Koko, a small, silver brood bitch with her varied-colored litter.

at birth. A pail of water near the whelping box is the easiest vehicle for this chore. Do not cull them immediately if they are the first to be born. Wait until the bitch is occupied with newly born normal pups and is about to again give birth before you stealthily extract the abnormal pup from the nest.

Usually the pups born first are the largest, particularly if the litter is a large one. This is due to the fact that the pups growing in the furthest part of the uteri horns sometimes get less nourishment than the others. But, once born and given equal opportunity to feast at nature's banquet, the smaller pups usually make a hasty size recovery and equal their formerly larger litter mates.

If the bitch whelps six pups or less and all seem normal and healthy no further culling is required. If she has a particularly large litter it does not pay, in the long run, to allow her to attempt to raise all the whelps without help. Let her keep six or seven of the best and cull the rest if she is a Standard. Miniature litters usually range from three to five, the latter number enough for the Minnie bitch to nurse. Toy Poodles will generally whelp from one to four pups and should not be allowed to feed more than four, a maximum of three being better.

You will find that, by culling large litters down to reasonable size, the pups retained will grow better and be healthier and possessed of more vitality than if you allow the entire, large litter to live.

Quiet puppies are healthy ones. Constant crying and squirming of the pups is a danger signal and a check should be made to see what ails them. Sometimes the trouble is *parasitic infestation, navel infection,* or possibly *coccidiosis.* It may be that the bitch is not providing enough milk and they are *hungry,* or perhaps they are *cold.* This latter cause, not generally taken into sober consideration by many breeders, can be a major reason for the weakening and death of puppies in cold climates during the winter season. Frequently a tiny, blind whelp will manage to squirm away from its dam and litter mates and unless its mother rescues it and brings it back, it can become fatally chilled before the breeder sees and helps it. The chill, combined with the pup's inability to nurse while not in contact with the mother, weakens it to the extent that it can no longer fight for position at the canine dining table provided by its dam and it goes down hill rapidly.

Puppies whelped in places where heat is lacking must be given survival aid. I advocate soft straw or hay bedding for the whelping box for this reason. If the bedding is deep enough the mother (sometimes with your aid) will form a

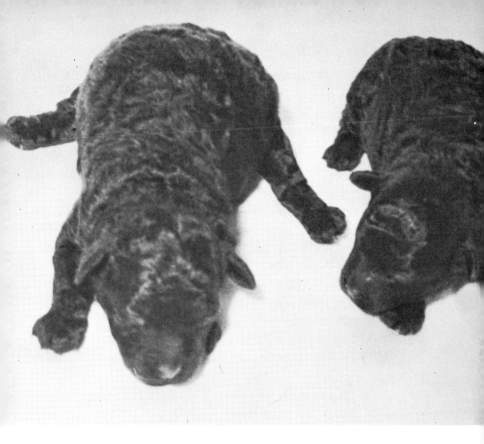

saucer in the middle of the straw or hay in which the puppies stay with little chance of moving away at this early age. The dam curls around this indentation giving the whelps easy access to her milk-laden udders. The pups are always close to each other sharing each other's body warmth.

Actual heat can be provided through the medium of any kind of coal stove, gas, or electric heater. Or an electric bulb (preferably infra-red) can be rigged up with an extension and an inexpensive green shade, to hang over the whelping box.

A new electric heating pad developed by the Goodyear Company offers a very definite solution to the problem of lack of heat in the kennel, pen or whelping box. This vinyl 24 by 33 inch pad, called the *Pliotherm Kennel Heater*, is easily installed, easily cleaned, and probably the best answer to keeping puppies in the nest warm.

There is nothing much you can do for the pups in the first few days except to examine the navels to see that no infection has set in (the cord left after the dam has chewed it rapidly dries up and drops off), and to remove the dew claws both on the front and rear legs. Of course the puppies' tails must be docked and this should be done on the third to fifth day after birth. Exactly half the tail must be removed. When your veterinarian attends to this mild amputation he can remove the dewclaws, too. If you elect to do the latter chore yourself they should be removed on the second day after birth with the aid of a pair of ordinary manicuring scissors. A small pip of blood will appear at the site of the removed dew claw and the pup will emit a wee cry. After the extra toes are removed return the pup to its mother. She will lick the tiny wound and keep it clean so that it will heal rapidly. If you feel that you are competent enough to

Ch. Crikora Commotion, handled by Jane Kamp to Best In Show at the Newtown Kennel Club, 1959. Owned by Mrs. J. Donald Duncan, this lovely Miniature was picked by judge Mrs. Paul Silvernail.

also handle the tail docking chore yourself, do it before the fifth day. As a matter of fact the third day after the puppies' birth is best since they have little sensation in their caudal appendages at this time but rapidly acquire feeling by the time they are eight or nine days old.

Use properly sterilized surgical scissors and have a styptic solution handy to stop any flow of blood, though a few moments pressure on the wound with wadded medicated cotton is usually all that is necessary. Make sure you have found the right place to amputate and that it is at the juncture of two vertebrae. Pull the skin of the tail back toward the body and cut. Dust a bit of antibiotic powder on the site of the cut and return the baby to the nest. The bitch should be removed during the docking and kept away from the pups for about an hour.

Check the tail ends for infection until they are completely

A Standard from Hawaii, owned by Mr. and Mrs. Henry J. Kaiser. The white, Tambarine De La Fontaine, winning at Westminster, 1960.

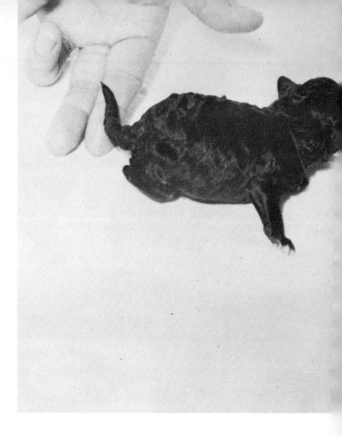

healed though, if they are properly done, there is little danger of infection. The pups will, in all probability, begin nursing on the mother as soon as she returns to the whelping box and the little tail ends will heal rapidly and without any trouble.

If, for one reason or another, the mother cannot feed the puppies I do *not* recommend that you attempt to do the job yourself. If, under these circumstances, it is possible to find a foster mother for the pups your troubles are over. Most lactating bitches will readily take to puppies other than their own if the new babies are first prepared by spreading some of the foster mother's milk over their tiny bodies. The foster mother will lick them clean and welcome them to her nest. If your bitch's litter is too large and you wish to keep and raise all the puppies, again the foster mother plan is the best.

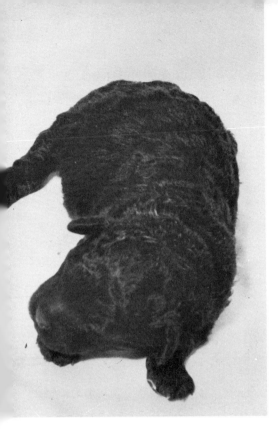

Two Poodle puppies from the same litter. Note the difference in size, a not unusual occurence in Toy Poodles due to crossing to Miniatures for type.

If you cannot find a foster bitch and decide to hand raise the litter you must remember that the most important requirement of newborn pups is proper food. Puppies are all belly and instinct and little more. They must be fed well and frequently. What formula can we feed these mites that will most closely approach the combined ingredients that nature provides them from their mother's breasts? Not pure cow's milk, as we can see at a glance by comparing the composition of the two liquids.

	Fat	*Protein*	*Carbohydrate*	*Ash*	*Water*
DOG	11.2	5.7	3.1	1.3	78.7
COW	4.0	3.8	4.1	0.7	86.2

But, since bovine is the only milk available, we must use it as a base and *modify* it to more closely approach bitch's milk. To do so we must specifically increase the fat and protein content. This can be accomplished by adding melted sweet butter to the milk. A little cream and meat blood will bring up the protein content, the cream also adding some fat.

Another, and perhaps even better formula utilizes *Pelargon*, a Nestlé's spray-dried, acidified and homogenized modified milk product. As a substitute for Pelargon, if it is not available, use any other fortified, spray-dried baby milk product. To one ounce of the modified milk product add one ounce of fresh cream. Pour six ounces of water by volume into this mixture and blend with electric mixer or egg beater until smooth. Large amounts can be mixed employing the same basic proportions and kept refrigerated until used.

Yet a third way to feed just-born puppies is to purchase a *prepared modified milk*, especially made for orphan puppies, which is commercially available and very much worth while.

Goat's milk is said to be rich in all the necessary nutrients a puppy needs for early growth.

Whichever formula you use must be fed five to six times a day and, when fed, must be warmed to body heat. Many puppies refuse to accept a formula that has not been warmed to just the right temperature. Do *not* add lime water, glucose or dextrose to the formula, for by doing so you are modifying in the wrong direction. These are canine puppies, not human babies. Avoid using an eye dropper for feeding unless you put a drop at a time on the puppy's tongue and make sure he swallows it, a tedious business and one that is too long drawn out to be sensible when feeding a litter. Inhaling milk fed from a dropper can cause pneumonia and death. It is best to use a bottle and nipple. A regular size

The proper milk formula must be understood if orphan puppies are to be fed properly. If mixed by the breeder-owner, modification in the correct direction must be made.

baby's bottle and nipple for pups the size of large Standards, and a doll's bottle and small nipple for Minnie and Toy pups.

The puppies should be fed the following amounts of formula.

PUPPY WEIGHT	AMOUNT OF FORMULA
3 oz.	$\frac{3}{4}$ teaspoonful
5 oz.	$1\frac{1}{2}$ teaspoonsful
8 oz.	$\frac{1}{2}$ oz.
12 oz.	1 oz.
1 lb.	$1\frac{1}{2}$ oz.
2 lbs.	2 oz.
3 lbs.	$2\frac{3}{4}$ oz.

Note: *The above amounts are to be provided at each feeding and are approximate, since puppy capacity varies as does human.*

The easiest way to feed orphan puppies is through the use of a tube which is pushed down, through the mouth and

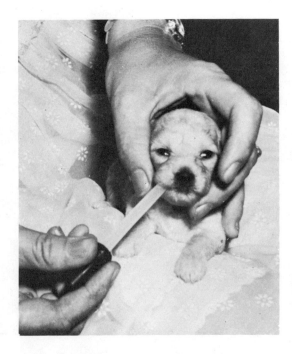

Feeding a tiny, young Poodle puppy supplementary vitamins. The administration of such extra elements must be done slowly, giving the tiny tot time to swallow the liquid.

Ch. Poodhall Gus, owned by Poodhall Kennels, taking a B.I.S. The Miniature is being handled by Hans Brunotte; judge is James Trullinger.

into the stomach. Use a number 10 French tube and a large syringe. Use Esbilac or any good bitch milk replacer. Feed 3 to 4 times daily, 20 cc. to 25 cc. per one pound of puppy. Be sure that the milk is kept at a 90° heat while feeding. 1 cc. of formula equals 1 calorie and it is necessary to feed 60 calories per pound of dog a day.

Today the Fading Puppy Syndrome or Puppy Septicemia, is well known to most breeders. During the first week various bacterial agents are the cause. After the first ten days, herpesvirus takes its toll up until the puppies are about three weeks of age. Puppies in the nest become weak, cry constantly, their skin wrinkles and dehydration occurs. The tiny stomachs of the whelps are evidently painful to the touch and, as breeders so often describe it, they seem to "fade away, one by one," and die in from 12 to 18 hours. The temperature of the stricken pup is generally, and surprisingly, normal. Protect the pups from stress conditions which help to initiate this syndrome, such as chills and an unsanitary environment.

27

To treat puppies that show even the faintest signs of being affected by Fading Puppy Syndrome, follow the ensuing program:

1. Raise temperature in whelping box to a minimum of 80°F.

2. Feed Esbilac or a replacer milk formula if there is any question as to the quality or quantity of the mother's milk.

Weighing a puppy helps you keep track of both its
health and food intake. It is especially important
when the puppy is being fed by hand.

3. Initiate supplementary feedings of raw liver juice
every 8 hours.
4. Give antibiotic (pediatric) drops (especially chloromy-
cetin or tetrocyclin) every 8 hours.
5. 2 to 3 cc. gamma globulin (concentrated serum) is of
great help in combating this killer of pups.

Give the puppies this treatment for from 4 to 5 days. The
recovery rate is excellent for puppies that survive the first
48 hours, especially if the disease is of bacterial origin.

If you encounter this syndrome in your whelping box and
lose the first pup it is advisable to have your veterinarian
perform an autopsy on the puppy and have cultures made
from any pathological organs, especially the liver, lungs
and intestines so that specific antibiotic medication can be
employed. The cost of such a procedure is but a fraction of
the value of one good puppy and may be instrumental in
saving the lives of the rest of the litter.

Many of these infections are transferred interuterine,
therefore a culture of uterine discharges, just before whelping or, preferably, at the beginning of the next heat period,
may identify the causative organism and, with proper treatment of your bitch, fading puppies may be eliminated and
even improvement in fertility achieved.

Let us hope that you will not have to hand feed your
litter. That the bitch is healthy and has plenty of milk. If
so it is best not to handle the pups much or allow them too
many visitors, Both mother and babies need peace and
quiet. Don't allow the bitch to spend all her time with the
whelps. She will need exercise and a rest from her brood
several times a day.

A well cared for and fed bitch, her udders filled with rich milk, is the best beginning toward healthy maturity for the pups.

chapter 3

WEANING THE POODLE PUPPY

Under normal circumstances it is best to begin supplementary feeding when the puppies are from $2\frac{1}{2}$ to 3 weeks old. Watch the whelps carefully when they nurse to be sure that they are getting enough milk from the mother to fill their bellies. If they hang on to a nipple, sucking enthusiastically and fall asleep, replete and satisfied, you can be sure that the bitch is providing them with maximum nourishment. But if they move frantically from one teat to another, sucking and searching, and their stomachs do not fill up, you will know that the bitch is no longer supplying them with enough milk for their growth and well-being.

Often when a bitch has a small litter of one or two pups her milk will begin to disappear much earlier than if she had a full litter to feed. If the mother has been bred too often without a rest her milk may go before it should. Even if the mother has enough milk to continue to feed the whelps substantially she will often engage in an instinctive and natural action when the litter is from $2\frac{1}{2}$ to 3 weeks old. She will regurgitate her stomach contents of partially digested food for the puppies to eat, thus serving notice, in her own way, that weaning time has arrived. If you have begun supplementary feeding in time, this action by the bitch will seldom occur.

To begin the process of weaning use any one of the formulas advocated in the last chapter for orphan puppies. Pour some of this liquid mixture in a shallow pan after heating to body temperature. Use only enough of the milk mix to cover the bottom of the pan. With one hand hold the pan just below the puppy's chin and, with the other hand, grasp him gently by the head just behind the ears and without exerting force dip his chin and lips into the pan. Release his head immediately and he will lick his lips and like the taste of the liquid he finds there. Speak to him quietly and in an encouraging tone as you repeat the process. Sometimes a puppy will begin to lap the pan milk after the first contact, sometimes it will be necessary to repeat the performance several times. You might find it necessary to hold the pup's chin in the pan until he begins to lap.

Be very careful not to pour too much of the milk mixture into the pan, or to push the puppy's head too far into the liquid. It is imperative that the pup's nose is held clear of the new food so that he will not breathe in the liquid or clog his nasal passages with the milk. If this occurs the whelp becomes frightened, eyes the pan with distrust, and the process of weaning becomes more drawn out and exasperating.

Repeat the process with each puppy until all have begun to lap of their own free will. It will be necessary to hold the pan at chin level for the pups during the first few feedings. But once they become expert at eating, or lapping, from the pan it can be put down on the floor. Of course they will crowd and step in it and smear themselves and their litter mates with the pan's contents. But they will also become more proficient in the process of eating from a pan which is the ultimate goal.

Feed the mixture twice a day for the first two days. By the end of that time the act of pan feeding will have become a conditioned routine. It is then time to add fat and some solids to their diet. They cannot yet chew so any solids added should break down into tiny pieces to form a heavy cream consistency when fed.

Puppies grow best on *milk, meat, fat* and *cereal* diets. Growth is attained through proteins mainly, but proteins differ, so that puppies fed on vegetable protein diets will not grow and thrive as well as those fed animal proteins. Vitamins E and K (one source is alfalfa meal) are essential to the pup's well being and must appear in adequate amounts in the diet. Remember that 70% of the youngster's energy is derived from fat intake, so supply this food element generously in the ration. In experiments, puppies on fat-free diets developed deficiency symptoms characterized by enemia, weight loss, dull coats, loss of vitality, and finally, death. Fat alone could not cure the advanced manifestation of the condition, indicating that some metabolic process was disturbed when complete fat removal in the diet was resorted to. But feeding butterfat plus folacin resulted in dramatic cures. Fat also acts as a vehicle for

Two top Miniatures, Ch. Tedwin's Two Step, Ted Young, Jr. owner-handler, and Mrs. Lewis Garlick's, Ch. Summercourt Square Dancer of Fircot, handled by Anne Rogers. The judge is Virgil Johnson.

This Miniature male is Touchstone Top Kick, owned by Touchstone Kennels and handled here by Anne Rogers. Judging is Miss Marjorie Siebern.

carrying the vitamins A, D, K, E. It slows digestion so that the animal gets all the nourishment possible from its food and helps in many other ways to keep a puppy, or fully grown dog, healthy and vigorous. To give your puppy all the virtues inherent in fat he should have 20 to 30% incorporated in his diet.

Practically every breeder you meet has their own weaning and after-weaning diet. The basic necessary element in any diet is balance. And a properly balanced food must be one that produces growth, health and vitality. There are fine commercial puppy foods on the market, in grain form, to which one need only add milk and fat. Or one can purchase grain human baby food such as Pablum, Ceravim, or those advertised as "high protein" and "fortified" children's foods. These, too, must be modified to fit the dietary needs of canine babies.

A fine little Toy owned by Mrs. Peter Frelinghuysen.
Walter Morris is handling Ch. Nibroc Gary, as
judge, Miss Virginia Sivori awards him Best Toy.

The author uses a mixture of rolled oats and wheat as the basic cereal. To this, while it is cooking, is added dried, powdered eggs, rendered fat (beef fat, lard, butter, crisco, chicken, etc.), ground beef, a little salt, and powdered milk. After this mixture has been cooked and cooled, a small amount of a vitamin and mineral supplement powder is added, thoroughly mixed in and the food poured into quart jars and refrigerated.

To make it ready for immediate use, the necessary amount is spooned out into the food pan, ground, raw meat is added (ground beef hearts, tongue, tripe, and a small percentage of liver), to increase the amount fed by about 25%, and evaporated milk mixed with water. The milk and water mixture is heated and, when added to the solid mix, heats it all to the proper temperature. When mixed the food has the consistency of very heavy cream. This consistency is gradually changed to a thicker, more viscous mix of porridge-like texture by the time the pups are 4 weeks old. Feed 3 helpings of the basic diet and two meals of milk.

By the time the litter is 5 weeks old a good finely ground grain dog or puppy food is gradually introduced to the basic diet. When the pups have become $6\frac{1}{2}$ to 8 weeks old, the original formula has been eliminated and they are fed the grain food with fat and raw meat, with milk and meat broths to give the proper consistency. Give 3 feedings of mix and one of milk.

A valuable adjunct to the puppy's diet is a good *feeding oil* (such as Dietol) or a fish liver concentrate oil. A drop in the lip pocket of each pup the day after birth and each day for a week, to be followed by 2 drops until weaning when the oil can be added to the food fed. Be very careful and do not overdo the feeding of any supplementary dietary oils or you may provoke the very kind (in appearance) of bone trouble you are trying to prevent by their use.

Toy, and even Miniature Poodle breeders, can rely heavily on the many canned and jarred *baby foods* on the market with small amounts of vitamin and mineral supplements added. Many Poodle breeders like to add yeast tablets to the feeding for Vitamin B. Two can be given to Standards, one for Minnies and a half tablet for Toys. Standards should be fed the diet recommended so that they will grow large and healthy. Miniatures and Toys, though they should be kept to their smaller size, must still be fed the same diet for their health, vitality, and future breeding worth.

Writing here of feeding reminds the author of a litter of pups he raised in Spain, on the Andalusian coast near Malaga. There was no dog food to be had and all the ingredients had to be bought raw and prepared from scratch. Wheat and lentils had to be soaked overnight to soften them enough for use. Meat was highly priced and scarce so I purchased

Wendell Sammet, handling the Miniature Poodle,
Ledahof Brazen Brat, owned by Jerry Silberg.

spleen, lungs, tripe and dried blood (the latter cooked and fashioned into blocks). The dried blood was wonderful for the pups. For both mother and pups I found it necessary to cook huge pots of the ingredients listed above to which I added vegetables, rice, olive oil and beef suet. Cod liver oil and powdered calcium phosphate could be purchased in a "farmacia."

Incidently, the veterinarians in that section of the country know little about dogs and have no serums for the dread viral or bacterial diseases. It was necessary for me to send a hurry cry for help to my veterinarian son, Allan, who immediately dispatched a "care" package with all that was necessary to keep the pups healthy and free from disease and worm infestation.

During the time we are occupied with weaning and feeding the pups we must not forget that there are other chores to be done. The puppies' nails should be kept clipped down with a manicure scissors so that they will not scratch the eyes of their litter mates in play. Their eyes will have

Dracest's Merri Minx, owned by Anna M. Drake and Cora Swackhammer. The photo shows this fine Toy going up under judge, Mrs. Lida Delmont.

Mrs. Sherman Hoyt awards best Miniature puppy to Woodland's Snow Flake, owner-handler, Mrs. Douglas R. Adams. Note the puppy clip.

opened when they were from a week to 10 days old and will be blue until they later change to their true brown color.

When the pups are 3½ weeks old a fecal check should be made by your veterinarian to ascertain if they have worms (and most puppies do), and what kind. If they are infested with worms, worm them *immediately*. If the worms have made them unthrifty do not attempt to build them up before ridding them of the parasitic infestation. After the worms are gone they will speedily return to normal health and plumpness.

Also, before the pups are completely weaned, and preferably while they are still feeding at the dam's breasts, it is wise to consult with your veterinarian about a planned series of protective inoculations and vaccinations. A new distemper serum is available which can be given to puppies at a very early age, even while still nursing. This serum (a human measles vaccine), given by intramuscular inoculation, is not affected by the natural immunity the puppies have

39

Barkhaven's Matara, a Minature owned by Sondern
Kennels, taking a Best Non Sporting win under
Frank Foster Davis. Anne Rogers is handling.

while imbibing their mother's milk, an immunity which makes the regular immunization vaccines negative.

This new vaccine is effective until the puppy has gone beyond all the important phases of early growth and, when he is about six months old he can be given the regular immunization vaccine for distemper. Incidently, the worms most puppies are heir to are the common round worms. Piperazine is less toxic than most worm medicines and the puppy can be fed normally, so this class of drugs can be recommended for round worms whose larvae in the bloodstream of the mother bitch often cross the placenta to infect the pup before birth.

You will find further information about your puppy's health and feeding in later chapters.

Most people worry about whether their pup is gaining

Mrs. Watson Hoos puts the Standard, Ch. Alfonco
von der Goldenen Kette, up to Best In Show.
Owned by Clairedale and Pennyworth Kennels, he
is being handled to this fine win by Bob Forsyth.

enough. One way to tell is by observing their overall condition, their plumpness and vitality. Another way is by
weighing the pups and keeping a record of their gains.
From six weeks of age to full growth a satisfactory average
gain per week for a Toy is $1\frac{1}{2}$ to 3 ounces, a Miniature
about 6 ounces, and a Standard at least a pound (and
generally more) each week.

Remember also to introduce your pup to *water* as a
beverage at an early age. At first they don't seem to see it or
know what it is, but they soon learn to lap it up just as they
do their milk and milk-mixed food and it is a valuable,
mineral-rich adjunct to their diet.

A quartette of English Poodles arriving at Old
Horticultural Hall, Westminster, to compete in the
International Poodle Club Show. There is one Toy
and three Miniatures and they are all owned by
Lady Stanier. Looking slightly rough at the moment
they will be groomed and barbered to the Queen's
taste before entering the ring in competition, you
may be sure of that.

chapter 4

FEEDING THE POODLE PUPPY

In a previous chapter (3) we learned quite a bit about feeding puppies during the process of weaning. But there is still a good deal to learn about the foods and feeding methods you must employ to bring your puppy to healthy, robust maturity.

There are certain factors that will retard puppy growth that we must be cognizant of if we would defeat disaster. Some pups that have been doing very well suddenly stop their precipitous rate of growth, or lose their appetites which causes their growth rate to slow down almost to a halt.

When this occurs we must immediately find the cause and correct it. The growth of puppies is an explosive thing that must reach completion in a comparatively short space of time. Children have eighteen or more years to grow to full maturity, or until the skeletal structure reaches maximum growth. Standard Poodle puppies show a skeletal freeze at about 9 or 10 months of age, Miniatures at about 8 months, and Toys at 7 months.

If anything happens to the puppy in those early months to slow or stop its growth and, whatever the cause may be, continues for any length of time, the puppy will never mature to his full genetic worth.

Worms are the first thought when the pup or puppies begin to do poorly. Sometimes worms can be detected in the stool, sometimes not, unless put under a microscope where the eggs can be seen and identified. Another cause of unthriftiness can be disease. If either of these causes is the reason for the pup's decline your veterinarian should be consulted at once and either the disease that is the causative agent identified and treated, or the worms, if they are the culprits, identified and eradicated by specific medicines or expellents.

Puppies will generally pick up and swallow anything that they find, and this can result in bad damage to internal organs and/or death if the foreign bodies they swallowed were any of the various poisons found in any household. This tendency to chew and swallow things other than food can also result in surgery to remove stones, wood, or other foreign bodies that have lodged in the intestines.

Lice can also cause loss of appetite and finally death if not eliminated. If enough of these tiny leeches infest a puppy they will cause anemia along with loss of appetite with death as the end result. Examine your puppies carefully if they go off their food or fail to gain, to make certain that the common dog louse is not the cause. If it is, de-lousing powder is the immediate answer to your problem with added vitamins, proteins and some liver, raw or cooked, added to the diet for about a week until the whelps are back to normal.

A *change of diet* can also put your pup off his feed with an accompanying weight loss. It is always better, therefore, to attempt to keep the diet unchanged as much as possible with any alterations or additives gradually introduced so there will be no abrupt difference in taste or texture of the food. Frequently (as a matter of fact, almost always), a pup bought from a breeder and brought to a strange home by the new owner, goes off his feed and quits gaining as he should. This is most often due to the fact that a change in diet is made by the new owner. It is best, therefore, for the purchaser of a puppy to duplicate the diet to which the puppy is accustomed with as much fidelity as is possible.

Above, the great little Toy, Ch. Silhou-jette's Snow
Sprite, owned by Martha Jane Ablett and handled
here to B.I.S. by Wendell Sammet. Below, taking
Non-Sporting group under George Owen, the
Standard Poodle, Ch. Estid Ingenue of Sterncrest,
owned by Dr. and Mrs. Joseph P. Murphy is
handled by Frank Sabella.

Another reason for loss of appetite in this case is because the pup misses its litter mates and the familiar environment into which it had been born.

Sometimes puppies who do not show gain are born with intussusceptions, which means that an area of the intestines have telescoped. Surgery is the only answer to this problem, for the pups are unable to digest their food and are also in pain.

One inescapable reason for weight loss in puppies is teething. Inevitably the time comes when your puppy loses

Judge Percy Roberts awarding Best Toy to Ch. Pixdown Little Bit, owned by Pixdown Kennels and handled to the win by Howard Nygood.

his baby teeth and replaces them with an adult set. This will occur at about 15 weeks of age, and for approximately six weeks it will continue until the puppy has all his new teeth. During this period the gums of the canine youngster are swollen and sore and the act of eating becomes a painful experience. As a result, for about a week, the pup will eat very little and his weight gain will slow almost to a stop. At the end of this first week of teething the pup has generally become accustomed to sore gums, ignores them, and eats with the same gusto as he did previously.

If, for any other reason than those listed above, your pup or puppies do not seem to be thrifty and do not exhibit the healthy appetites and gains in weight that you think they should, consult your veterinarian and let him, a professional, cope with your problem.

From puppyhood to full growth, it is a mistake at any time to drastically change the animal's diet or eating habits. These habits you shape in the pup when he is young and constantly hungry, and should be adhered to throughout the animal's lifetime. Change turns dogs into finicky eaters, and finicky eaters are an abomination. Dogs do not need

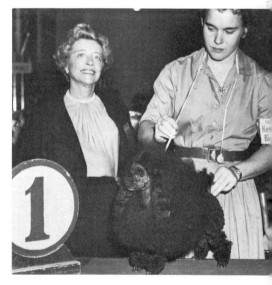

Best Toy Poodle under Mrs. Milton Erlanger, is won by Norgate Too Spicey. Owned by Lorraine Rothstein, this splendid little Toy is being handled by Jane Kamp.

variety in their diets as do humans. Your dog can smell separately all the various ingredients that are mixed into his food pan, so that each meal, though the same as the last, is nevertheless a delicious variety of intriguing odors and tastes, a diverse and delectable banquet fit for a king . . . and what Poodle is not a king in his own home?

To realistically approach the problem of feeding for maximum health and strength and vitality in maturity, we must weigh the canine's needs against the food substances available to us.

47

These tiny, little Poodle pups
are only a few days old.
Soon their eyes will open
and they will see their
world for the first time.
Once weaned they must be
fed correctly if they are to
attain to healthy and happy
maturity.

The Poodle is a carnivore, a flesh eater. His teeth are not made for grinding, they are chiefly fashioned for tearing and severing. This has led to the erroneous conclusion that the dog must be fed mostly on a muscle meat diet in order to prosper, and this idea came, of course, from the observation of the feeding habits of the wild canines, the wolves, dingoes, jackals, wild dogs, and foxes.

But, these feral carnivores consume the entire body of their prey, not just the muscle meat alone. First these wild hunters lap the victim's blood, then they tear open the stomach pouch and consume the stomach and its contents composed of predigested vegetable matter (the main prey of these wild cousins of your dog being the hoofed, herbiverous animals, and small mammals and birds). They then feast on the liver, heart, kidneys, lungs, spleen, and fat-encrusted intestines. They crush and consume bones and marrow, fatty meat, connective tissue and, finally, the muscle meat. They slake their thirst at the nearest stream after their meal and, through the agency of one hoofed animal (deer, sheep, calf, goat, colt, kid, etc.) have absorbed minerals and assorted proteins, fats, fatty acids and carbohydrates, vitamins and roughage for proper laxation. From the sun that shone on them as they ate, and from the water they drank afterward, they absorbed supplementary vitamins and minerals. To supply the same essentials to your dog in a form which you can easily purchase is the answer to his dietary needs.

For health, vigor, and normal growth puppies and adult dogs must be fed all the food essentials, and these necessary ingredients can be found on the shelves of your local grocery store. There you can buy all the natural sources of the dietary necessities in the list that follows.

1. *PROTEIN:* meat, dairy products, eggs, soybeans.
2. *FAT:* butter, cream, lard, oils, milk, cream cheese, suet, fatty meat.

3. *CARBOHYDRATES:* cereals, vegetables, honey, syrups.

4. *VITAMIN A:* greens, peas, beans, broccoli, asparagus, eggs, milk.

5. *VITAMIN D:* fish liver oils, eggs, fortified milk, some fish.

6. *THIAMINE:* vegetables, whole grains, eggs, milk, yeast, muscle and organ meats.

7. *RIBOFLAVIN:* milk, *liver,* egg yolk, yeast, wheat germ, beef, chicken.

8. *NIACIN:* milk, lean meats, liver, yeast.

9. *ASCORBIC ACID:* tomatoes, citrus fruits (not necessary for dogs).

10. *IRON, CALCIUM AND PHOSPHORUS:* milk and products, eggs, blood, liver, oatmeal, bone marrow, vegetables.

The first three listed essentials complement each other and compose the basic nutritional needs. Proteins build new body tissues and are composed of amino acids, which differ in combination with the different proteins. All living cells are composed of protein molecules so proteins are essentially the basic elements of life itself. Carbohydrates furnish the fuel for growth and energy, and fat produces heat which becomes energy and enables the dog to store energy against emergency. Vitamins and minerals, in general, act as regulators of cell activity. All other vitamins, the B-Complex, E and K, are contained in a well-rounded diet, as well as the so-called vitamin F, which is actually the unsaturated fatty acids.

Milk, perhaps the most complete of all natural foods, lacks in iron content. But puppies, unless plagued by hookworms or lice, are born with enough iron stored away to last for the several weeks of milk diet they must endure until just past weaning time when they get their first solid food. The meat in that food will supply them with all the

51

Best Miniature at the International K. C. of
Chicago, 1965, Ch. Round Table's Cognac, owned
by Round Table Kennels, and handled to this win
by John Brennan under judge, Henry Stoecker.

iron they need. Puppies, when very young, need vitamins
E and K. They manufacture their own E as they do vitamin
C, and the K they get in their mother's milk, and also in any
balanced diet fed after weaning.

All the *proteins, vitamins* and *minerals* are important to
the puppy's health. But any of the balanced diets recommended in this book, or meat, milk, fat, a sprinkling of
vitamin and mineral supplement, and a good manufactured
dog or puppy food as a base, will supply all of these nutritional elements the pup needs.

Some of the trace minerals may become of greater importance in the future than we ever dreamed they would be.
Just recently *zinc*, important to growth, but thought to
only be necessary in so small an amount in the mammalian

body that its presence is recorded as a "trace," has been found in the research laboratory (by a fortunate accident) to have another, and very important, function. It almost miraculously aids in the growth of tissue, so that the healing of wounds becomes a far quicker process than ever before thought possible through the agency of added zinc.

Canned, or *pudding foods*, are good. But remember that they already contain the liquids necessary to mix the ingredients. They are especially good to feed when traveling with your dog, or when at a dog show. Many Poodle owners, especially of Minnies and Toys, have had excellent results from a canned food diet.

The canned meat, chicken, lamb, etc., for dogs is very good to add to the basic milk, cereal, fat, mix. *Biscuits* are

The lovely Silver, Ch. Hermcrest Jamal, sired by Ch. Freeland's Flashlight and out of Hermcrest Hermione. The judge is Marjorie Siebern.

good to clean the puppy's teeth, help his gums and give him some nourishment and food value, but a good deal of the vitamin and mineral content of a biscuit has been destroyed by baking, so they cannot be considered a balanced diet. Some of the kibbled biscuits have this same disadvantage. But the *grain foods* and *pellet type foods* are very fine balanced dog foods. Add to a good grain food some fat (20% to 30%), milk, meat and meat broths, with a small sprinkling of a powdered vitamin and mineral supplement, and you can be sure that you are feeding your dog well. Some animals prefer something more to chew than a grain food provides and, for them, the *pellet type food* (grain food to which a binding agent has been added) is the answer.

The author prefers to add vitamins and minerals to the diet in as natural a form as possible. To this end I mix Brewer's yeast, alfalfa meal, green ground edible bone meal, salt, and a bit of bicarbonate of soda (the latter to neutralize stomach acidity). Instead of Brewer's yeast, irradiated yeast can be used. As already mentioned, commercially prepared vitamin and mineral supplements such as Vionate, Paltone, Pervinal, etc., are excellent.

Please heed this warning relative to the usage of supplements: do not overdo them! An overdose of most vitamins will be carried away in the bloodstream and not harm the individual. But there are some vitamins, or their vehicles, that can prove very harmful if given in too large a dose over a period of time. Cod liver oil, used as a vehicle for vitamin D, if given in excess over a period of time, can cause toxicity and malformation of the bones similar in clinical aspect to the very disease (rickets) that it is used to prevent. A fish liver oil concentrate is much better to use.

Calcium and phosphorus in pure chemical form must be handled with care when used in the puppy's diet. Toxic conditions can be caused by an overabundance of this material in the bloodstream.

Water is one of the elementary dietary essentials. Considering the fact that the dog's body is approximately 70% water it isn't difficult to understand the importance of this staple to the animal's well being.

Water is one of the major sources of necessary minerals, helps to regulate the dog's temperature, and prevents dehydration. It is also the least expensive element of the animal's diet, so supply it freely, particularly in warm weather. But, when you are housebreaking your puppy only give water under supervision. A puppy who has water available will drink all day, and a puppy who drinks all day will piddle all day.

If you are feeding only one or two puppies or dogs, table scraps can be included in the diet. But be sure that, for the most part, and day after day, the basic diet is used to prevent that bane of the dog owner's existence—a finicky eater.

The consistency of the food you feed young puppies must be soft and creamy. As they grow older the texture should thicken and take on greater body. At six months a wet, sloppy mixture is not relished by most dogs, so the consistency of the food should be thicker and dryer.

If, because of a change of diet or a liking for some specific food or table scrap not provided, your puppy refuses to eat, remove the food pan and do not offer it to him until the next feeding time. Be sure, of course, that the pup is healthy and is not refusing food because he is ill. He may refuse the second or even the third time offered the food pan. But hunger will eventually drive him to eat when it becomes acute enough and he realizes his hunger strike has done him no good.

Do not ever leave the food pan in front of a puppy who will not eat, for more than 15 minutes. If he hasn't touched his food by then, remove the pan and offer it again at the next meal time. Remember that during these tender weeks you are aiding the puppy to form the food habits that will remain with him all his life, so shape them to your will and

The fine Standard bitch Clarion Demitasse, being
presented with a top award by Percy Roberts. She
is owned by Jaronda Kennels.

convenience, not his. He is also, through the food pan, being conditioned to obey you in other ways which will prove fruitful during later training.

Wash all pans and utensils used in the puppy's feeding immediately after usage. Each time you feed the pan should be completely clean and never display dried particles of food along the edges left from the last feeding. All food given the pup or puppies must be fresh and refrigerated if perishable. Make sure that nothing mixed in the food has turned sour since the last time used.

Following is a chart indicating the age of the puppy and the consistency of the food it should be fed.

AGE	FOOD
weaning; 2½ weeks (*feed twice a day*)	*Liquid, orphan puppy formula (for 2 days)*
weaning (*feed 3 times a day*)	*Heavy creamy consistency. Add solids 2 meals a day of mix, one of milk fortified.*
4 weeks	*Thicker, porridge consistency mix. 2 solid meals, 2 of milk.*
5 weeks	*Add grain puppy food to mix. 3 meals of mix, 2 of milk.*
6½ to 8 weeks	*Original mix eliminated. Feed grain puppy food, meat, fat, milk and meat broths. Milk meal.*
3 months to 8 months	*3 meals of mix. Eliminate milk meal. At 6 months begin to add adult dog food, kibbled or grain.*

Supplements can be added to the food mix at 4 or 5 weeks. Food should be served at blood heat until 3 months. After that make sure food has had chill removed and is served at room temperature. Water can be supplied after each meal from 4 weeks on. After housebreaking water should be made available at all times. From 8 to 18 months, feed 2 hearty meals. Fully adult dogs usually require only one meal a day.

chapter 5

SELECTING THE POODLE PUPPY

Time passes quickly when you watch a litter grow. If you are the breeder you have certainly not wasted that time. You have watched the puppies in the litter carefully, while they ate, while they ran around, walked and played. You have probably centered your interest on one particular puppy, or perhaps two that are difficult to choose between, for this pup or these two puppies show the greatest promise of any in the litter.

As the breeder you should know all there is to know about their genetic background, what faults and what virtues are

The night a Toy Poodle went to Best-In-Show at the famous Westminster K. C. Show, a night to remember for Ch. Wilbur White Swan and his owner, Bertha Smith. It would be nice if we could all select a dog of this quality from a litter.

prevalent in the strains represented by the dam and the sire you selected to produce this litter. You can look for these faults and virtues in the puppies to see if hidden recessives have linked in this breeding and become visible in the whelps.

You also have had the advantage of knowing the sire and probably have seen other of his get from different bitches so that you know what he can pass on to his puppies.

The puppy you select as outstanding in the litter you will either keep, if it is of the right sex for you, or you will sell for a higher price to someone who is looking for a potential show dog.

If you are the prospective *buyer* of a puppy you lack the above advantages enjoyed by the breeder. But the strange part about this whole business of picking a young puppy from a litter is that the novice buyer *sometimes* stands as good a chance of getting the best pup as the experienced breeder does. The reason for this seemingly incongruous statement lies in the fact that, assuming the litter is of excellent breeding and well cared for, there will probably be more than one puppy in the litter that will appear to be a potential winner at eight to ten weeks of age.

Most prospective Poodle puppy purchasers are not as interested in getting a show type animal as buyers of other breeds. If you are just looking for one of the most intelligent, loving, willing and wonderful companions and pet dogs that money can buy, the most important items you will be concerned with are health and color.

Find out who is breeding good Poodles, healthy and intelligent, within easy driving distance and check into the breeder's integrity, and attempt to see other stock that has been produced by this breeder. If you can, select several breeders and visit them all, as well as your local pet shop, making mental notes about the quality of the stock, the kind of people they are, and the cleanliness of the kennel area. When you have made up your mind where you want to buy your pup, go back and see what young stock they have on hand or which bitches will soon whelp.

Of course, with Poodles, the prospective purchaser has *three* sizes and a wide variety of *colors* to choose from. The official standard for all three sizes is exactly the same. In other words, the Standard Poodle, the Miniature and the Toy, should all look practically alike. The only difference is in the eventual size that they will attain upon maturity. The Standard Poodle must be over 15 inches at the withers when fully grown, the Miniature 15 inches maximum and 10 inches minimum, and the Toy 10 inches or under.

Actually, the Miniature is the only one that is fairly squeezed into a definite size pattern. Standards have no upper limit and often attain quite a large size, so if you are going to select a Standard puppy, make sure that it will mature into approximately the size you want. I have seen people who envisioned owning a 16 to 18 inch Standard, end up with a 25 inch curly giant.

To avoid the above, check the size of the parents and, if possible, the grandparents and other relatives of the puppy in which you are interested.

At left, the three recognized sizes for Poodles. To the far left is the Toy, in the middle the Miniature, and the Standard is on the right. The Black Toy is Ch Fieldstreams Valentine, the Brown Miniature is Ch. Cappoquin Bon Jongleur, and the White Standard is Ch. Puttencove Moonshine.

We have already established the size of the Miniature, but Minnies that are on the short side of the accepted size standard can seldom win at shows so it is sometimes possible to get a good buy on a fine puppy in the Miniature classification that looks as though it is going to be on the small side. It is also sometimes possible to buy at a good price, a Miniature puppy from very fine parentage whom the breeder realizes will go slightly over the 15 inch mark.

The same thing can be found in Toys. A good buy can be gotten if a Toy puppy is too big and will edge over the 10 inch mark. Even though this would make it a small Miniature, it should be bought reasonably, for the Toys seldom display the same classic type wanted in the Miniatures, despite the complete similarity in the official standard.

Poodles that are called *phantoms*, and *parti-colors*, can also be bought at a greater bargain than those of the normally recognized colors. Neither of these color variations (or patterns) are recognized by the A.K.C. as true Poodle colors, consequently animals of this coloring cannot be shown in competition. These are the puppies that are the first to be culled by many Poodle breeders. Actually these off-colored little tykes make just as intelligent and wonderful pets as do their correctly colored brethren.

The phantom Poodle is, instead of solid in color, marked or patterned like a Manchester Terrier or a Doberman Pinscher, in a symmetrical distribution of two solid colors, these colors being generally black and white or brown and white. Black and white phantoms are sometimes sold as grays by uninformed or unscrupulous dealers. To determine if a tiny puppy is a solid or a phantom, look beneath the tail. If it is a phantom you will see there a tiny triangle of white. If it is a solid this triangle will not be there. Parti-colored Poodles are born parti-colored, with an uneven distribution of either black or brown patches on a white ground. Though parti-color can actually come in all the colors the Poodle is heir to, with the colored patches against a white background,

At the top of the page is the Chocolate, Ch. Donna
of Westford-Ho, owned by Harmo Kennels,
handled by Bill Trainor, Judge L. Murr. Below is
the Apricot Miniature, Ch. Pixiecroft Sunbeam,
handled by Anne Rogers, owned by Mrs. Gardner
Cassatt. The judge is Haskell Schuffman. Best
Non-Sporting, Westminster K.C. Show, 1965.

the most commonly found are the black and brown partis.

The four basic colors that most Poodle breeders aim for are, white, black, brown and gray. White and black Poodles do not change from birth. The color should be solid and without blemish. Browns come in many shades, from the pale Champagnes to the deep Chocolate browns. Grays vary from deep steel-blue grays to pale silvers. These gray Poodles are born black and to determine if the puppy is black or gray examine the underside of the baby's paws. If the hair on the instep between the pads shows gray hair

The good, white Miniature, Ch. Tedwin's Top Billing.

the pup will mature into a gray. If the hairs on the instep are solid black, the puppy, too, will be solid black.

Sometimes, very frequently admittedly, but occasionally, a Poodle will change its color after maturity. I have known of a fine black Poodle of excellent ancestry who turned to a deep gray, and a gray who developed black spots on its back after maturity.

A Poodle puppy begins to show his true color ("*Clears his color*") at from two months to a year of age, but he might not be completely "cleared" until he is a year and a half old.

Above, the lovely Silver Toy Poodle owned by
Barbara Ann Woods. Below is a Best-In-Show
winning Brown Miniature Poodle, Ch. Harmo
Porgy, owned by Harmo Kennels.

Actually, there has been so much color crossing to get and hold type in Poodles that genetically the color picture of a good many Poodles is a puzzle, even to their breeders.

Regardless of what color you pick, be certain that the puppy has all that marvelous charm that the breed is known for, and pick the puppy that seems to fit your own temperament. As a matter of fact, you will quite often find that the puppy will pick you instead of vice versa.

In most kennels solid color is bred to solid color to avoid, if possible, the appearance of phantoms or parti-colored pups. And, if you feel that you must have a show type Poodle pup, then go to a breeder or kennel who specializes in top specimens of the breed and breeds specifically to produce show-worthy Poodles. It is best to bring with you, if you can, an experienced person whose knowledge of the breed you respect. Such an authority cannot guarantee to select the *champion* out of the litter, but can keep you from purchasing a puppy who has *obvious faults,* and they can select the best puppy in that particular litter at that particular time. This is, of course, no guarantee that some other puppy (or even puppies) in the litter will not, upon maturity, be better than your selection.

Sex is up to you. Females come in season twice a year and attract male dogs from near and far at these times. But they can also produce puppies and bring gain to you in various ways. Females are generally more loving and quicker to learn, and they do not roam from home, a failing of the male dog, particularly if there is a bitch in season in the neighborhood.

Male dogs can "burn" shrubbery when they urinate. They can be used for breeding, but it is easier to select a male owned by someone else for this purpose and pay a stud fee. If you don't have a male you will not be tempted to make a breeding that might not be just right. Instead you will find a male who *will* be "just right" for your bitch, to breed to. Of course if you have a male who is a very fine

Born black, this Miniature puppy is genetically a
Silver and its coat color is beginning to clear,
turning from black to the proper Silver color it will
attain completely with maturity.

producer or a top champion, you may reap a fair harvest in stud fees. If you want to breed Poodles, or start a kennel, buy the finest bitch you can. If you want a pet or companion, the matter of which sex to choose is in your hands.

In any of the three varieties look for a short back, a long neck, and Hackney Pony action. A well knuckled-up foot, a gay and happy tail and a degree of elegance throughout should be selected for. The puppy coat will not be tightly curled, so do not look for the "astrakhan" appearance until the adult coat comes in. Examine the mouth for a scissors bite, and look for a bright and mischievous eye, dark brown in color. The ears should be fairly low set and the legs straight in front and well let down in hocks behind. Look for an animal that has good, general physical balance.

When you have decided which sex you wish, have the puppies separated and only those from the sex you have decided upon left for you to choose from. This is best since males and females have slight physical differences due to their sex and it only confuses the purchaser if all the pups are running around.

If it is a male you have decided on, don't forget to examine him for sexual wholeness. The testicles should be in the scrotum and are, indeed, so small that they are difficult to find. It is therefore wise to have the seller guarantee, in writing, that the male puppy will not display orchidism (the lack of one or two testicles that have not descended) upon maturity.

With your puppy purchase you should receive a bill of sale that guarantees the puppy to be free of disease (or a health certificate), an A.K.C. registration slip, and a three generation pedigree. You should keep the puppy isolated from other dogs for a week to 10 days. The reason for this time limit is because most canine illnesses have an incubation period of from 5 to 10 days and, if the puppy becomes ill during this period, the disease was contracted in the seller's kennel or home, *not* the buyer's.

The initial buying cost of the puppy is small compared to the cost of feeding, caring for, and keeping the puppy healthy and happy during its lifetime, so don't balk at an extra few dollars on the purchase price for a better puppy. In the long run it could be a good investment.

Remember always to give your pup the opportunity to develop the character and intelligence for which the Poodle is justly famed. If you have children ask if the pup comes from a family that is fond of children. Many Poodle families possess this trait, especially Standards that have a good deal of German breeding behind them. Miniatures and Toys never display the puppy fat that Standards do, they are too active, so if puppies of these two (Miniature and Toy) sizes exhibit much distension of the stomach it can be due to worms.

Poodles want to become part of the family and are never quite happy unless they are given this privilege. They thrive on companionship and become terribly lonely if left alone for any length of time. Full of fun and harmless mischief they are nevertheless always sweet and companionable. They are one of the few breeds that have been bred specifically for intelligence for uncountable generations. Versatile and smart the Poodle has been used for many tasks over the years in many countries. It is up to you, the new owner of a specimen of this grand breed, to bring out all the many facets of your Poodle's personality, character and intelligence, and soon it will be more to you than just a dog, it will become the epitome of the perfect companion.

chapter 6

REARING THE
POODLE PUPPY

The little mites that you have bred and brought into the world, or the tiny puppy that you have bought and brought home, are or is completely dependent upon you for care.

Good husbandry pays off in dollars and cents, for clean, well cared-for puppies are generally healthy puppies free from the small ills that bring greater woes in their wake.

Healthy puppies are, in turn, more saleable and at better prices, and need less, expensive veterinarian care.

Puppies need *exercise* and *sleep*; a good deal of sleep as does any young mammal. They will, of course, begin to play with each other in the whelping box soon after their eyes are fully opened and they are able to move around with some assurance. But they need play in the fresh air as well. These outings relieve the monotony of the whelping box and its surroundings.

Select a warm, sunshiny day for their first introduction to the out-of-doors and provide them with a pen, so that they will not roam too far, if you do not have a kennel run for this purpose. This wire pen can be of heavy mesh chicken wire, about 3 feet high and with metal stakes at each corner. It should be set on grass. This can be the beginning of housebreaking, for the puppy will soon prefer to eliminate outside.

The puppy pen can be about 5 feet square for Standard puppies. 4 feet square is large enough for Miniature babies, and 3 feet for Toys. Standard pups can be given outdoor exercise in their pen even in winter. But it is best to allow Minnies and Toys outdoor pen time only when it is fairly warm.

Never take baby puppies in the streets or visiting. The only time the pup should leave the place where it was bred

Ch. Icarus Duke Otto, owned by Mrs. Robert Tranchin and handled by Jane Kamp, achieved Best-In-Show under Miss Anna K. Nicholas.

The Miniature, Ch. Adastra Magic Fame, going
Best-In-Show under George Owen. This
handsomely coated White is owned by Mrs.
Marguerite Tyson, and here handled by Maxine
Beam.

and born is when it is sold and brought to its new home.
Too many elements of illness and contagion to which it
has no resistance can be encountered by the small pup
removed from the environment to which it has adjusted.

Take the puppy out and put him in his pen (either indoors or out) for playtime, immediately after feeding.
Generally a half to three quarters of an hour of playtime
(particularly outdoors), will result in an hour to two hours
sleep. Puppies need this sleep so they must not be disturbed.
If they are young during the summertime when the sun is
high and hot, provide shade for them in the play pen. This
is easily accomplished by throwing a piece of canvas over
the top of the pen to shut out the rays of the sun from at
least half of the pen area.

While the puppies are young and ravenous with the hunger of all young, growing things, is the time to condition them to sharp sounds so they will not be sound-shy later. This can be done by making such sounds while they are eating. Actually, if you do a bit of hammering close to where the whelping box is when the pups are still nursing and haven't yet opened their eyes, they will become accustomed to sound, accepting it as a part of their environment. But, if you wait until later when they are pan feeding, keep the sounds fairly soft at first, then increase in volume and sharpness, so that the sharp sound of a hammer striking wood, the top of a pail hitting the floor, the quick clapping of hands, or the firing of a gun close to them will have no effect and they will continue their frantic feeding as though they hadn't heard a thing.

Though this is the type of training indulged in by gun-dog breeders, and we are not concerned here with gun or sporting dogs, it is nevertheless a necessity to accustom your pups to such noise so that they will not be sound-shy. You may possibly want to work your Standard in the field as a water dog, at which he will most probably do very well, due to his ancestry. If so, sureness to sound becomes an absolute necessity.

Feeding utensils should always be kept clean. Heavy aluminum or light pressed steel feeding and watering pans are best, since they are easily cleaned and do not chip as does agate and porcelain. Feed the pup or pups regularly at the same place and at the same time. Establish a friendly and quiet atmosphere during feeding and do *not* encourage the youngsters to play at this time. It is meal time and they must learn to apply themselves to the food pan without outside distraction.

Watch the puppies when they are eating. There are always the slow eaters or the less aggressive ones that get pushed aside and therefore fare less well at the feeding pan. If the litter is large enough it is best to separate them into

Jalen's Percette, being handled by Ben Burwell, is
owned by Allen C. Warder and Jane Speiser of
Jalen Kennels.

two groups, the aggressive, hearty eaters in one group, and the more timid, slow eaters in the other group. Or give extra attention to the slower ones and see that they get enough to eat or they will "go thin" and lack in substance and strength.

During hot weather, be certain that the pup has a constant supply of fresh, clean water. If water is not available at all times, provide it in quantity within an hour after feeding. There is a new lick-spout on the market, similar to the watering devices used for small laboratory animals, that will supply constant fresh water from a faucet without the necessity of pail or pan watering. The faucet to which this gadget is attached must, of necessity, be low enough so that the pup can reach it easily.

Accustom the puppies to being brushed and combed at an early age. Teach them to stand still at arm's length during the procedure. An ordinary hair brush of any kind can be used for very young puppies, and a good quality wire brush and a steel comb later. The head hair of your Poodle can be tied or bobbed to keep the hair from actually going into the eyes. Many Poodle owners do not care to shave the hair above the eyes, preferring to clip a small V between the eyes to allow some shade.

Every Poodle pup should have a run of its own, its sanctuary where it can rest or sleep, or merely keep out of mischief when you are not in the vicinity. An outdoor run for all sizes of Poodles can be so constructed. Of course tiny Toys, particularly of the "sleeve" variety, cannot survive in extremely cold weather in the out-of-doors. Still, even these little ones, if provided with a house small enough to be heated well by their body heat, can do all right for short periods of time outdoors, and particularly so if there is more than one of them and they can share their body heat inside the house.

A *portable run* can be used at first to give the pup or puppies exercise and sun outdoors. Such runs can be

Show stacking a young Poodle puppy. Gentle
handling such as this is excellent for the youngster,
teaching it early, correct deportment, and will
reap dividends later if the puppy matures into a
show-worthy animal.

bought in all sizes and are handy to have. Or you can build
your own, making it just high enough so that the pup can't
get over but not too high to prevent you from stepping
over into the pen. Metal stakes can be used for the corner
posts.

Small runs with attached houses can be built off the
ground and with wire bottoms for ease in cleaning, for
Minnies and Toys. Most owners of the latter varieties of
Poodles prefer a portable run or cage in the house in an
unused room or a warm cellar. In such case the flooring
should be surfaced with oilcloth or rubber as a base for
easy cleaning.

Your Poodle puppy should never be chained. Even a confining wire pen, such as the one shown above, is better than chaining your dog. This Poodle is getting fresh air and sunshine and waiting for the master to arrive, take him out of the pen and give him needed exercise.

Beds for your Poodle pup can be bought at any pet store. A metal frame bed is less likely to be chewed and ruined than a wickerware one. For the puppy a canvas mattress should be supplied. Later, when he has quit chewing, and to give more protection to elbows and coat, a softer mattress should be used.

It is this author's opinion that a puppy should never be chained up. That is why I so vehemently recommend the use of a run, either indoors or out. Incidently, a good sized Standard is a hardy animal, so don't baby him weatherwise. At the same time it must be understood that a dog that is kept in the house most of the time cannot stand cold as well as one that is generally kenneled outdoors.

The best surface for an outdoor run is open to argument. Many breeders have their own pet run surface that they claim is best. The easiest to take care of is a *cement* surface, but it can get quite hot underfoot for a pup during the summer months. I have always recommended a cement base with *building sand* on top. Stools are easily removed from the sand, it packs down nicely, and periodically it can be completely removed and a new sand surface provided. It is inexpensive as a surface and the cement underneath, when the sand is removed, can be burned or the surface washed down with disinfectants to destroy worms' eggs, etc.

Fencing the permanent run can be done in various ways and at different costs. Sections can be bought ready for erection, or you can use cedar posts and less expensive wire. It is up to you. Just be sure that the materials you use will not degenerate in a short time and have to be replaced. And see to it that the run wire is high enough to keep the puppy in when he's fully grown, and strong enough to hold him at maturity.

Don't bathe your young pup unless it is absolutely necessary. There are many dry shampoos on the market today that, coupled with a good grooming, will generally

A handsome young male
Silver Toy Poodle, still in a
puppy clip. This dog, Encore
Silver Showman, was a
show winner while still
under a year of age, so was
exhibited in the puppy trim.
Owner is Mrs. Jane Fitts,
Encore Poodles.

BASIE

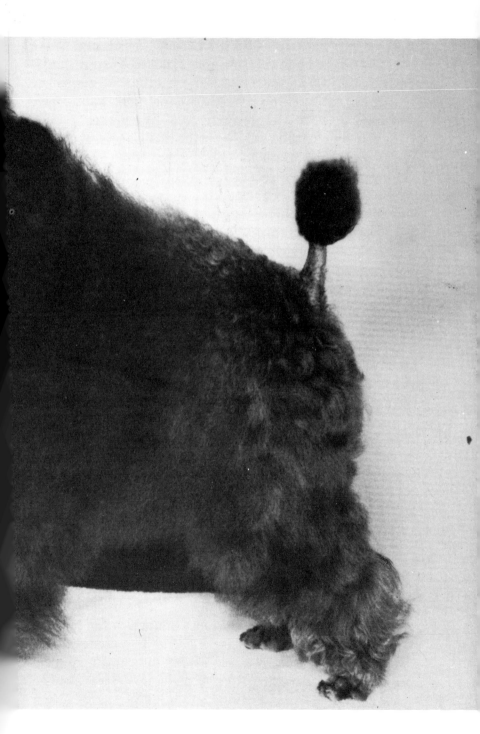

remove any dirt and keep your puppy clean and sweet smelling. If your pup gets into and is stained by paint, check the thinning agent and use it for removal, but remember that the agent must be removed by soap and warm water *immediately*. This is especially true of turpentine.

If you find it necessary to bathe the puppy, there are prepared, canned lathers, paste soaps that require no rinsing, and liquid detergents, all manufactured specifically for canine bathing. When older your Poodle should be bathed, "fluff" dried, and clipped, once a month.

Keep the puppy's toenails trimmed. This can be done with a manicure scissors while the puppy is young. Later, as the nail becomes tougher and more horny, the guillotine-type of nail clipper made especially for dogs should be used. Be careful not to cut too deeply. A flashlight held under the nail will enable you to see the dark area of the blood line so you can avoid cutting into it. If you should tap the blood supply in the nail, simply keep the puppy quiet until the bleeding stops. Munsel's solution or a styptic pencil will help. A regular dog file can be used to finish the nails. If a nail has bled from trimming do not file it for at least 24 hours. File from above with a downward, rounding stroke. If you live in the city and your pet gets plenty of exercise walking on cement sidewalks, its nail growth will probably be taken care of by the natural wearing off produced by the cement surface. If not, clipping will be in order.

Soft rib bones, dog biscuits, and some of the manufactured play-toys for puppies, will all help to prevent tartar from forming on your pup's teeth. A puppy begins to shed his baby teeth at about 14 weeks of age. Check the mouth frequently during this period. Sometimes you will find it necessary to pull a loose tooth out, which can be done with a small pair of electrician's pliers. The gums will be swollen and painful to some extent but, unlike human babies, puppies have little trouble teething.

When you purchase a puppy and bring it home, be sure

that you have everything prepared for the new addition to your family. Have pans for food and water ready, a special place where the new arrival can sleep in peace. And let him roam throughout the house to become acquainted with it.

Show your new Poodle puppy where his basket bed is and make sure that it is in a secluded spot where he can retire when tired of human company. Make sure it is not in a draft and is warm and comfortable. Until the pup is completely housebroken it may be wise to confine him to a specific area that can be easily cleaned, such as the bathroom.

Remember that the pup had lots of exercise when with his mother and his litter mates, but now he has no one to play with for his exercise but you, so you must supply this essential too. A thrown ball, toy, or stick that the pup has been trained to chase will give him the exercise he needs.

If you travel with the pup in hot weather, never leave him in a closed car in the sun alone. Death takes its grisly toll each summer of dogs so treated.

A periodic health check of your pup throughout his lifetime by your veterinarian can pay big mental and monetary dividends. Remember to bring a sample of his stool for analysis.

We must never forget that this pup needs mental as well as physical care. Other breeds can be stuck away in a kennel and make a life for themselves, but not Poodles. Your pup's character and mental health needs care as much as his physical being. Give him companionship and understanding and you will be paid many times over in love and devotion.

chapter 7

TRAINING THE POODLE PUPPY

All Poodle puppies must be trained so that they will conduct themselves in the manner expected of such well-born individuals. We are indeed lucky in that our pupil is of a breed of acknowledged superior intelligence. During this early training period when you are shaping the character and intelligence of your puppy into specific patterns of behavior you will also be fashioning a relationship between yourself and your dog that will endure throughout his life-time. You give the commands, and your puppy *must* obey. This is the simple formula for training.

The author does *not* believe in punishment as a means of training. I *do* believe in the reward system, but the reward I advocate does not necessarily need to be a tidbit or such

reward to the primary senses. A pat, a smile, a "well done," by his master is quite often all the reward that the puppy needs. With some pups, or under some circumstances, the tidbit reward may be necessary or desirable, and should then be used. But physical punishment, beating, whipping, or hurting the pup, is the act of a sadist and such a person should not train a dog, rather should they train themselves.

Actually using your hand, the leash, a broom, rolled up newspaper, or any other such vehicle for punishment or to show your displeasure to the puppy for any act he has committed, results in his fear of the object and of the act of training itself. If you slap and hurt him with your hand he will very likely become hand-shy. He can become leash-shy, broom-shy, etc., with the use of such objects by you to hurt him while conveying your displeasure. Rolled up newspaper as a punishment vehicle can make it impossible to housebreak him to paper, or can result in his attacking the paperboy at some later date.

The only reason for striking a dog is if he, with malice aforethought, bites. The only other reason to mete out physical pain is when, after all other methods fail, you must break your dog of car chasing. Then the water pistol with a weak solution of ammonia and water can be employed with the knowledge that it will certainly discomfort the dog but, with possible death as an alternative, is definitely the lesser of two evils.

Except for the above reasons, there is no excuse for using physical violence during the act of training a dog unless it is your last recourse and, if it is, then you must face the fact that you, *not* your dog, has failed, and that you are not able, or fit, to train a dog.

When you train a dog you do two things; you exert your will over the puppy and his actions and, in so doing, you *control* his conduct (the word "control" is the important element here). Secondly you condition the puppy to react to specific external stimuli.

The secret of complete control is *firmness*. Always be firm and insist that the puppy obey once he understands what it is you want him to do. The basis upon which the conditioning of the puppy to perform certain acts is founded is through exact and constant *repetition* of the stimulating factor. In other words, when you condition a puppy to perform a certain action through a command you have given him, you are causing him to form a habit pattern to which he will react *automatically* whenever he hears that specific command. But, to achieve exact results, the conditioning factor, the *command*, must always be the same, never varying in structure or tone. Therefore, if the command is, "Come, Duke!", never vary it to "Here, Duke!",

"Come on!" or any other grouping of words or sounds that mean the same thing to you . . . they won't to the pup. The command must always be, "Come, Duke!", delivered in the same way with the identical tonal quality every time it is used.

Other important elements of training are: keep training periods short, lengthen the time as the puppy grows older and has absorbed other commands, use sharp, short, easily understood words of command, approach the training period seriously, have a definite time for it when there will be no interruptions, select a training place where there is no outside activity that can steal the pup's attention from his training, censure the pup in a rebuking tone when he doesn't obey, and praise him or reward him with a tidbit when he obeys promptly.

The equipment necessary to train your pup is simple, unless you become enamoured of obedience work and go on to advanced training. You will need a chain choke collar and a long leash.

But, before you begin any formal training you can lay the basis for the pup's later deportment through the very important and initial job of puppy training, *housebreaking*. For this chore you need no collar or leash, merely knowledge and patience.

You will need to know that puppies urinate very soon after drinking milk or water, also when they have been brought into a warm room, particularly if brought from an area where it is colder. They will also wet directly after they have been awakened. Puppies defecate generally within a half hour after eating.

You will have to patiently watch the puppy until you become aware of the warning signs and movements that precede evacuation. When you see these signs pick the pup up *immediately* and rush him to the place you have assigned for these duties, indoors or out.

When the pup, by accident or design, goes where you

Consistency is the most important element leading to control, and control is completely necessary for successful training. If you don't wish your Poodle puppy to use the furniture be consistent in commanding him off it.

want him to, praise him extravagantly. Should he make one of his frequent mistakes, scold him, using both your voice and its tone to impart your displeasure. The simple word "No!" is adequate and a word he should learn and obey in diverse other circumstances during training. "Good boy," or "Good girl," as the case may be, delivered in an excruciatingly pleased voice, conveys your praise.

Whatever the material used underfoot in the whelping box or nest will be the substance upon which the puppy has learned to go and will seek afterward. Thus a puppy conditioned to go on paper in the nest will seek paper when out of the nest on which to do his duty, and will be readily paperbroken. If hay or straw was used in the whelping box it will be much easier to teach the puppy to go outdoors in grass.

A Poodle puppy that will mature into Standard Poodle size should be trained to use the out-of-doors. If you wish

Housebreaking is the nemesis of many dog owners.
Your Poodle puppy is highly intelligent and
basically clean so it should be no great chore to
housebreak the tyke. Oral punishment and praise
are the necessary useful elements.

to housebreak it to paper first the pup should be brought
to the paper after meals, when awakening from sleep, after
drinking, etc. If you can catch him in the act, grab him up
and rush him to the paper. A loud "No!" or "Shame!",
will frequently cause a cessation of the act which will continue when you have him on the paper and tell him what a
"Good boy!" he is. Poodles are exceedingly smart and
quick to learn so that it will not take many lessons before
he understands and obeys.

Miniatures and Toys, particularly the latter, if owned in
any section of the country where inclement weather can be
expected during the winter months, are generally paper or
box trained. Box training is handled in the same manner as
paper training, by being alert, bringing the puppy to the
box when he is about to void and using the words of praise
or condemnation, whichever fits the behavior of the moment.

The box can be filled with sawdust, layers of paper, paper scraps, or sand.

Never rub his nose in his excreta as a form of punishment or training, and *never* scold him unless you catch him in the act. A few seconds later he will have forgotten what he has done and punishment will only bewilder him for he will not have the slightest idea of why he is being chastised.

If a paper-broken puppy is to be trained to go outdoors, simply remove the *soiled* paper from the house and anchor it outdoors with stones so that it will not blow away, then bring your puppy to it. Once he begins to use it outside, then you must commence cutting down on its size until nothing of it is left (after a priod of 8 or 10 days), and the pup is using the bare ground.

A lot of grief can be avoided by confining the pup to one room until he is thoroughly housebroken, particularly at night. This should be a room with a linoleum or tile floor for easy cleaning, probably the bathroom. If he is house-broken during the day but makes mistakes at night, tie him close to his bed, or confine him to a dog house within the room; few dogs will soil their beds or sleeping quarters. If you must leave the pup alone for any length of time, con-fine him to a limited area which includes his bed and the paper or box.

The use of human baby suppositories can aid you in timing the evacuation process and controlling that time. Injection of the suppository generally brings quick results.

Another trick used in paper breaking is to confine the pup to a small room and cover the floor with paper. After he has formed the habit of going on the paper begin to remove a piece day by day until only one piece remains. This can then be taken beyond the room with a closed door in between and only a small edge of the paper projecting into the pup's room. The pup, wanting to go, will see the edge of paper and begin to whine and he will be, as of that moment, housebroken to paper wherever you wish to place it.

Assuming that the puppy is housebroken let us now return to the area of training deportment. Our first task will be to collar and leash train the puppy. To this end you must purchase a narrow, cheap, flat leather collar and allow him to wear it constantly and become used to it. After a day or two attach a piece of cord to the collar long enough to reach the ground. Don't let him play with the cord, just let him drag it around and become used to it so that he will be partially leash-broken by the time you attach the leash and gently lead him about.

Once he accepts collar and leash make him follow you, using short, gentle jerks on the leash to make him move with you. Call his name to get his attention, then add the word, "Heel!" Soon he will trot along freely at your left side (always on your *left* side) on a loose leash, and you will be praising him with the inevitable, "Good boy!"

Every time you feed your pup, call him with a "Come!" Eating is a pleasurable experience and you are *conditioning* him to come to you freely. Later, with the long leash attached to his collar, get as far away from him as the length of the leash and call, "Come!", and in no time he will respond. It is generally best to preface every command with the use of the pup's name. He learns his name early and by using it in this manner you immediately catch his attention. Always use short jerks on the leash, *never* a long pull.

To make the puppy sit, hold your hand under his chin to prop up his foreparts and with your other hand press down on his rump forcing his hindquarters to go down, at the same time using the vocal command, "Peter, sit!" Augment this positive training by voicing the same command quietly whenever you see the pup about to sit of its own accord.

Once trained to "sit" upon command, both positive and negative approaches can be utilized to teach him to lie down. Here the command is "Down!" and the puppy, already in the "Sit" position is either pushed down in front or the front legs pulled forward so that the forepart lowers to the

When your Poodle becomes older and you begin serious training, the "Sit" is one of the most important of training positions, for from it stems most other training movements. Below the trainer is giving his Poodle pupil the "Stand-stay" command, orally and with the proper hand gesture. This training command is particularly good for the dog that is shown in conformation classes as well as worked in obedience.

The well trained Poodle is a pleasure to own.
Completely under control at all times and with
gentlemanly conduct instilled during the training
process, your Poodle can be taken anywhere you
go, thus sharing in your daily activity.

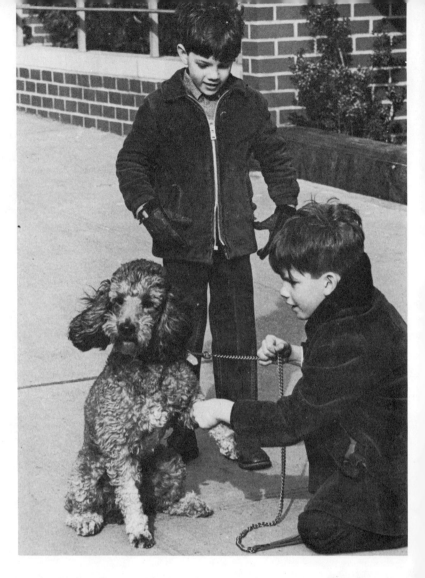

ground or floor. Again the negative approach can be utilized through observation and taking advantage of the pup's natural inclination to lie down and giving him the command when he does.

When you have housebroken your puppy, trained him to "come," "heel", "sit," and "down" upon command, you have accomplished all you can until you begin serious training when he is about 6 months of age. For this advanced training the author recommends that a book on training be purchased that is devoted wholly, not in part as is this book, to this subject.*

All that you have read in this chapter in reference to training is basic, specifically aimed at training the young puppy; a sort of kindergarten course. That is why the "sit!" and "down" commands can be taught off leash. When serious training begins with the older puppy, the leash is always used until advancement has been such that the dog will work accurately and with verve and dependability off leash. Teaching the very young puppy the necessary few basic commands should not be done with the grim, rigid, business-like air employed later in serious training. The puppy should nevertheless obey the simple commands with alacrity once they are learned, for you are establishing, in these tender weeks, the control necessary for earnest training to come.

Later, with the puppy leashed and at your left side, the act of training him to "sit," "heel," "down," etc., will be an accomplished fact and only promptness and precision must be learned. This also helps the pupil to move with ease into the much more rigid regime of real training for he already knows how to perform some of the acts and he has been conditioned to obey and to be controlled by your voice and will to perform certain exercises.

Poodles love to work and learn to do things, so give your puppy the opportunity to exhibit his inbred intelligence. Train him, for you will be amazed at how quickly your Poodle will learn and ask for more.

*HOW TO TRAIN YOUR DOG, is recommended by the editor, a fully comprehensive, easily followed book on training by the same author, Ernest H. Hart.

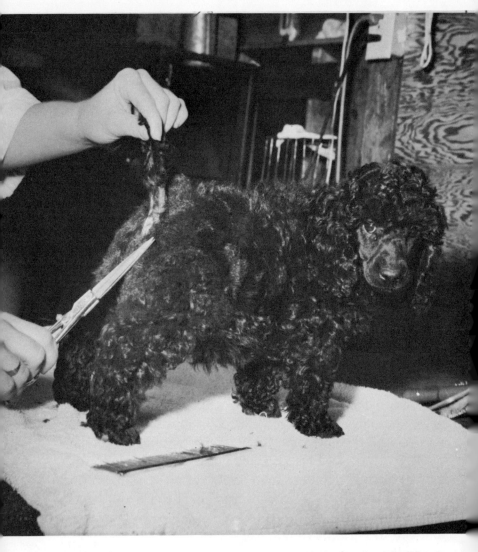

To keep your Poodle looking neat and handsome, barbering is necessary even for a puppy. This youngster is being trimmed in a puppy clip. The pup's face has already been clipped and the hair around the tail is being scissored to neatness.

chapter 8

CLIPPING YOUR POODLE PUPPY

Clipping your Poodle can be almost a fine art or, in the case of a pet, it can be easily done by almost any member of the family. A great majority of Poodle owners do not even attempt to clip their own animals, and are content to bring them to canine beauty parlors where they will be bathed, groomed (teeth and toenails attended to as well as coat), and clipped. But costs mount up for this kind of service over a period of years, and it is easy, with a little knowledge and practice, to clip and groom your own puppy.

There will, of course, be the initial cost of equipment to consider. You will have a comb and brush, but will need a pair of barber's shears and an electric clipper. Coat grooming, and washing, have been covered in another chapter, so we will concern ourselves only with the clipping and trimming of the coat. You will need a table or stand of some kind on which to place the puppy when you clip him, and the height should be such that it will allow you to work in comfort. To this bench should be fastened a reverse "L" shaped bar, the horizontal arm of which should be high enough to allow about a foot of space above the head of your Poodle when he stands on the bench. A light leash or chain attached to the arm and fastened to the Pup's collar will help steady him and hold him, leaving your hands free for the actual work of clipping.

The electric small animal clipper comes in several brands and can range in price for from $10 to $50 according to

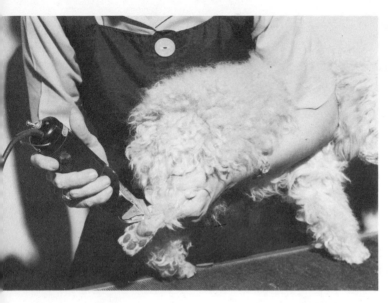

Above; using the clipper on the Poodle's feet. Below; the sides of the face and the neck are being clipped close, the muzzle has already been clipped clean.

quality. If your dog is just a pet and you merely wish to clip him to keep him looking nice and trim around the house, the cheaper clippers will do the job efficiently. If you have a kennel of many dogs, or if you are a show ring addict and must trim your dogs for exhibition, then the better and more costly electric clipper should be invested in.

Regardless of which clipper you choose, get one with interchangeable heads so that you can use blades of different sizes. The Oster Small Animal Clipper is perhaps most commonly used by veterinarians, kennel owners and professional handlers. The blade numbers listed below are those used in this clipper.

Blade numbers 15, 10 and 5 will be the most useful to the average Poodle owner. For you who are about to attempt clipping for the first time, the number 15 blade is recommended. It is a blade for general usage since it is less likely to nick or irritate the skin of your Poodle when being used by unskilled hands.

A number 9 or 10 blade is most often recommended for the Dutch clip, especially for Toys. A number 30 blade will cut too close to ever be used by anyone but a professional. The higher the number the closer the blade will clip. A fine blade will cut the hair to within 1/32" of the skin, while a skip-tooth blade allows long, shaggy coats to be fed with greater rapidity to the cutting edge and is therefore particularly useful in clipping Standards.

The first time you introduce your Poodle to the clipper is extremely important. He might fear the sound and feel of it and form a habit-pattern of nervousness that will make clipping a chore. Show him the clipper and talk lightly about it so he will know that it is nothing to be afraid of. Click it off and on a few times and tell him it is all in fun. Finally, with the clippers *off*, run it through his coat and around his head a few times until he shows that he has no fear of it whatsoever. After a couple of such sessions you can gently begin the actual job of clipping.

Very young puppies have their faces trimmed or "shaped up" slightly. Just trim the cheeks with your clipper, and trim around the eyes with scissors. Remember to always cut *with* the lay of the coat, not against it. The latter practice causes irritation, skin burns, and cuts unless it is done by an expert, for there are certain areas where the cut must be very close when preparing a dog for the show ring, and a professional, using the skill of many years, can cut against the grain without harm to your dog, to get the desired results.

Remember to hold the *flat* of the clipper blade against the surface you are clipping. If you tip it forward you will dig in and cause unsightly cut marks. Any time after the puppy is three months of age you can begin to clip. Up to a year of age there are only three clips that should interest you, the Puppy Clip, the Kennel Clip, and the Dutch (or Royal Dutch) Clip.

Begin by clipping the feet, base of tail, and foreface. Be content with only using the clippers this first time you clip your puppy. Once both of you have gained confidence you can graduate to the use of other tools. Incidently, when using the scissors to shape around the eyes always keep the points angled away from the dog's optics, for a quick move by the dog could be disastrous if the shears were pointing toward his eyes.

In the *Puppy Clip* the face, feet and the bottom half of the tail are clipped clean. The tail pompon is shaped round with the shears and the hair on the head, ears, neck, body and legs is combed out and trimmed slightly (with a racy slope from the head to the tail), with the scissors. This clip is, at maturity, easily converted by show-minded owners, into the standard English Saddle or Continental Clips that the animal must wear in the show ring.

The *Kennel Clip* is easily accomplished and easy to maintain. Basically it is the same as the Puppy Clip, except that the hair on the neck and body is cropped much closer

Hall's Golden Rambler, a nine month old puppy, is
shown winning while still wearing a puppy trim.
The youngster, a Standard, is owned by Margaret
R. Hall, and is here being handled by Donna
Rogers.

This Grey Poodle, a miniature, is sporting the popular Dutch trim. This is not a recognized show clip, but is greatly favored by pet Poodle owners.

(1″ to 2″ in length) to show the lovely, tight Persian-lamb curls the breed is so noted for. The hair on the ears, head (topknot), tail and legs are left as they are in the Puppy Clip, but with the leg hair trimmed a bit closer so that it will be approximately double the length of the body hair.

The *Dutch Clip* is the favorite clip of pet dog owners. Somehow this trim seems to be the personification of the Poodle's character shaped to physical aspect, and particularly is this so for the Miniature and Toy sizes.

To accomplish the Royal Dutch Clip, the feet, neck, middle body band, all of the ear but the tassel, all of the face except the mustache are clipped clean. The bottom half of the tail, and a path along the middle of the back, are also clipped close and clean. The facial whiskers are left

Ch. Alekai Pokoi, going to B.I.S. under judge Peter Knoop. Handled by Wendell Sammet, this fine White dog took many top awards. She is shown in an English Saddle clip, a favorite show clip for mature dogs.

unclipped and combed forward, and the topknot is trimmed to a sloping "V" on the back of the neck. The ear tassels are combed out and down. The rest of the body left unclipped, is trimmed with shears to remove any raggedness from the outline.

In this Dutch Clip the operator can indulge in modifications if so minded. Many owners clean the muzzle completely, clipping the mustache off but leaving the rest of the trim alone. The neck "V" can be eliminated and the hindquarters cut to resemble the classic English Saddle Clip. This Dutch Clip lends itself readily to improvisation.

The Poodle's head and face are the most difficult to clip.

Hold the dog's muzzle with one hand while you work with the clippers in the other. When clipping the muzzle hold the dog's head above the foreface. In the Royal Dutch, where the mustache is to be allowed to stay, the hand should be held under the jaw with the fingers curled up around the muzzle to protect the area not to be clipped.

The lips and the feet are both sensitive and should be carefully done. The scissors is handy in removing hair from between the toes that the clipper misses. Also use the shears to trim long hair at the bottom of the feet between the pads.

When clipping the underbelly of a Toy or Miniature, roll him over on his back, or standing behind him, lift the back legs so he is standing on his front legs alone, then run the clippers along the belly line.

Make sure that the puppy is clean before you clip him. If he isn't, wash him first and comb him out before clipping. Take care of your clippers. Keep them oiled and cleaned, and they will last a long time and give you good service.

You may make a mess of the first couple of clips, but persevere and soon you will get the hang of it and save yourself all those clipping fees besides taking pride in your accomplishment. You can keep your dog well tailored so that he will always look clean and handsome and, instead of being a tangled, unsavory mess, or a constant monetary liability, he will "walk in beauty."

Another top Standard Poodle, the bitch, Ch. Lady Margaret of Belle Glen. She is owned by Mrs. James Cosden and is being handled, in the photo at the right, by Richard Bauer. Lady Margaret is wearing another show trim, the Continental Clip, well liked for mature Poodles and coming into particular favor at this time.

chapter 9

THE POODLE PUPPY'S HEALTH

Let me make something clear at the beginning of this chapter; you are not a veterinarian and therefore you are not really capable of treating your puppy for illness any more than you, a layman, are capable of treating your child when it is sick. But, there are many ways in which you can help your pup retain its health, and it is important that you are cognizant of the symptoms of disease and ill-health so that treatment can begin in time.

Fleas and *lice* can spread worm eggs, skin disease, and make your puppy anemic. *Ticks* are a nuisance to dogs and pups in many areas. Dust your pup with a good flea, tick and louse powder, or use a good spray. Chlorinated hydrocarbons (DDT, chlordane, dieldrin, etc.), are long-lasting and excellent.

Your dog should be kept clean and healthy particularly if it is to be around children. A healthy dog is a happy one and a little common sense on your part, combined with the help of your veterinarian, can keep him healthy.

Mites cause mange (demodectic or red mange, and sarcoptic or white mange), and ear mite infection (generally called canker). Mange mites cause balding, redness, rawness, and irritation. The coat falls out leaving denuded areas. Earmites cause the dog to shake his head and scratch delicately at the seat of infection. A crumbly wax forms inside the ear that has a distinct odor. All three of these conditions must be treated by a veterinarian.

Parasitic infestation internally is still a great cause of

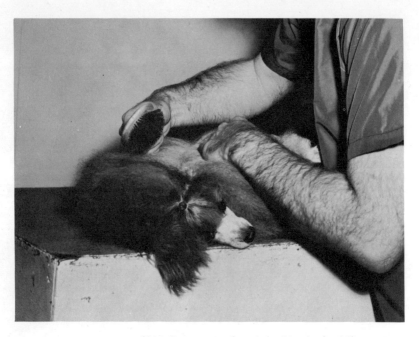

Skin disease can be nipped in the bud if you are observant during the process of grooming your Poodle. It is always best to check disease before it becomes deeply rooted.

concern to dog and puppy owners. A fecal analysis is necessary always to determine the kind of worms present and specific medicine employed to get rid of them.

Roundworms are the most common worms found in puppies. Potbellies, coughing and general unthriftiness are the symptoms. Frequently these yellowish-white worms that are shaped like a garden worm, can be seen in the puppy's stool. There are many different species and they can bring death to your puppy through the toxins they discharge within the pup and the presence of their larvae in important organs of the pup's body.

There are many drugs that can be employed to rid your puppy of these deadly pests, including N-butyl-chloride, tetrachloroethylene and the piperazines, the latter drug easier to use and less dangerous than most others.

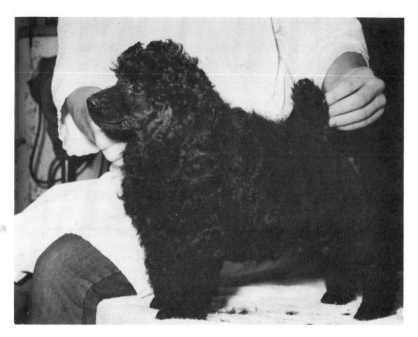

Most puppies have worms, but there are
particular drugs for the elimination of specific
kinds of worms. Your veterinarian will identify and
eradicate those your dog has.

To the first two drugs mentioned above add tolkuene for
the elimination of hookworms. Disophenol, in subcutaneous
injection, is the newest and most effective hookworm treatment.

New formula Vermiplex capsules are a specific for the
eradication of round, hook and tapeworms, and are very
effective.

If the infestation has been abnormally heavy, blood trans-
fusion may be necessary for quick recovery. Add liver, raw
meat and iron tonics to the diet of the hookworm victim.

Whipworms are a very definite contributing factor in
lowering the resistance of the pup to the onslaught of other
infections. Most worm medicines that are used for other
worms will kill whipworms, too. But some invade the
cecum and these are hard to reach. Phtalofyne, administered

by either oral tablets or intravenous injection, is an effective eradicator of these tiny worms.

Tapeworms and *heartworms* are two other helminths that cause tremendous damage and death to pups unless gotten rid of quickly. Tapeworms succumb to the drug arecolene, and heartworm is treated with a wide range of drugs including the arsenicals, antimony compounds, and caracide.

These worms are dangerous and should not be treated with home cures. A fecal examination should be made for identification and the correct drugs used to expel the worms. Usually two series of treatments are necessary, for eggs still left in the animal after treatment can hatch and cause the same trouble over again. Dietary supplementation will also be necessary to build up the puppy victim of internal parasites.

Another disease, *coccidiosis*, caused by a tiny protozoan, is also very dangerous to puppies. A severe case often proves fatal. Loose and bloody stools as well as general unthriftiness is indicative of the presence of this disease. The reason coccidiosis is so dangerous is because the puppy is infected over and over again. Strict sanitation and supportive treatment of good nutrition, utilizing fat, milk, bone ash and kaopectate, with added dextrose and calcium is all that can be done in the way of treatment. There is no known drug as yet that is a specific for this disease, though fragmentary clinical evidence seems to indicate that sulfamethazine may give some control over canine coccidiosis.

Skin diseases, other than those caused by mange mites, are the eczemas and ringworm. Ringworm is a fungus infection and is contagious to humans (athletes foot is ringworm infection). In puppies ringworm generally appears as a round or oval spot from which the hair has fallen. Iodine glycerine or a fungicide such as girseofulvin are definite cures for this condition.

Of recent origin is a new drug to retard the spread of, and to cure, fungus. It is a locally applied fungicide named

Tinactin, is colorless, odorless, stainless and liquid, and seems to be equally effective against almost every form of fungus infection.

The appellation "eczema" covers a multitude of skin sins. There are wet and dry forms of this common skin disorder. Both forms cause a loss of hair at the site and irritate and itch. Eczemas are probably originated by various fungi and bacteria and aggravated by flea allergic conditions and self trauma. An overall dip, employing specific liquid medication combined with the application of a good skin remedy that contains a fungicide, is the best way to bring these diseases under control. Your veterinarian may also use injectable or oral anti-inflammatory drugs for supplementary treatment.

Your puppy may display small eruptions on his belly or eyelids, paws and muzzle. The rash is caused by a bacterial infection of skin glands and hair follicles. Wash the affected areas with alcohol or witch hazel and apply a healing lotion or powder.

Deficiency conditions are caused by lack of necessary dietary elements in the food, or some condition or illness that keeps the puppy from making full use of the necessary ingredients supplied. Anemia, rickets, etc., are deficiency diseases and, like all such diseases, are characterized by unthriftiness in one or more phases. The cure is simple; supply the necessary food factors that are missing in the diet.

In the group of *bacterial diseases* we find many dangerous illnesses. The mortality rate is high and treatment should be left in the hands of your veterinarian. Leptospirosis, tetanus, pneumonia, tonsillitis, are all diseases in this category.

Leptospirosis is spread by rats and by the urine of infected dogs, and can do great harm to the affected animal's kidneys. Vaccines are employed as a preventative measure.

Tetanus is lockjaw bacteria and exceedingly poisonous.

Clean, well fed, well groomed, these fine Standards mirror the good ownership and care to which they are heir. Animals such as these are a pleasure to own and live with.

Deep wounds must be thoroughly disinfected and an anti-toxin given the puppy.

Tonsillitis can be of either bacterial or viral origin and is sometimes a symptom of some other disease. The tonsils are enlarged and reddened and the affected pup has a poor appetite, vomits and shows optic discharge. Penicillin and some of the "wonder" drugs (mycins, mycetins) are utilized as treatment.

Pneumonia affects the lungs and symptoms are general

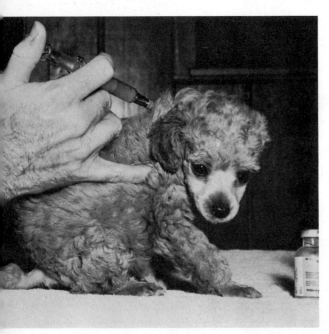

Have your veterinarian set up a program of protective vaccinations for your puppy.

unthriftiness and shallow and rapid respiration. Antibiotics and sulfa drugs, combined with a pneumonia jacket, is standard treatment.

The dread *viral diseases* are caused by the smallest organisms known to man. They live in cells and often attack the nerve tissues. Secondary bacterial infections cause complications and are treated with several of the "wonder" drugs. Nursing of the stricken animal is important.

Rabies, distemper and infectious hepatitis are viral

Good and canny breeding, coupled with smart
husbandry and veterinary care, aid in molding
winning Poodles like these. Above: Ch. Estid Aristo,
owned by the late Col. Ferguson. Below: the
Standards, Bel Tor St. Ay Better Mousetrap and
Bel Tor Head of the Class, both owned by
Mrs. Jesse Mason.

diseases, and every puppy should be, indeed must be, immunized against them. Various methods of immunization have been developed, combining several vaccines in one. The wise thing to do is to consult your veterinarian and allow him to prepare a program of immunization for your puppy. New vaccines offer a combination of distemper, hepatitis and leptospirosis protection. Immunity, in some cases, was thought to be for life, but recent studies would indicate that for full immunity booster shots should be given every six months to a year.

Fits in pups are symptoms of disease rather than illness itself. Your veterinarian should be consulted. *Diarrhea* can also be included in this category as a symptom rather than a disease. If only a simple intestinal disturbance a tightening agent such as Kaopectate should be given along with boiled rice, hard-boiled eggs, bone ash, kibbles, crackers or dog biscuits. Withhold water and substitute corn syrup dissolved in boiled milk to prevent dehydration.

Constipation is generally caused by diet. Introduce laxative elements into the diet such as, stewed tomatoes, buttermilk, whey, bran, etc., and a bland physic such as milk of magnesia should be given.

To administer liquid medicine make the puppy sit, raise his head and you will find a pocket at the corner of his mouth. Hold the pocket open and pour the medication in. A small bottle used as a vehicle for the dosage makes accomplishment easier.

To adminster pills again raise the head of the patient and by putting pressure on the cheeks of the pup just behind the lip edges where the teeth come together inside the mouth, force the mouth to open. Push the pills down the throat as far as possible, using the eraser end of a pencil if necessary, then quickly shut the mouth and hold it shut firmly but not too tightly. When the tip of the tongue emerges from the front of the pup's mouth you will know that the pills have been swallowed.

Beaujeu Richeleu Ruffles above, owned by Mrs. D. Goldstein. Right; Midcrest Ice-A-Rama, owner-handler, Miss D. Valerie Reid.

An ordinary rectal thermometer can be used to take your dog's temperature. The arrow that points to normal human temperature, 98.6 degrees, should be disregarded. Normal puppy temperature varies between $101\frac{1}{2}$ to 102 degrees, and sometimes higher if the pup is excited. Normal temperature for a grown dog is 101 degrees.

In applying ointment to the eye, simply pull the lower lid out and squeeze a small amount of ointment into the pocket thus produced.

If your pup becomes badly injured, quickly snap a leash on his collar and get him to your veterinarian as fast as you can. Prompt action by you and your veterinarian can save the life of the puppy that has become so much a part of your life.

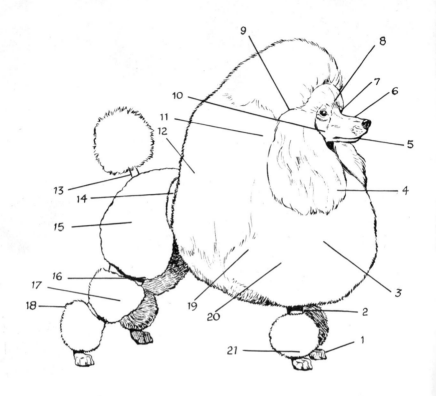

EXTERNAL PARTS OF THE POODLE

1. Feet 2. Forelegs 3. Chest 4. Ear 5. Lips 6. Muzzle
7. Eye 8. Skull 9. Top of Ear 10. Cheek 11. Neck
12. Back 13. Tail 14. Loin 15. Thigh 16. Stifle
17. Second Thigh 18. Hock (point) 19. Ribbing
20. Elbow 21. Pastern

chapter 10

THE POODLE STANDARD

General Appearance, Carriage and Condition—That of a very active, intelligent and elegant-looking dog, squarely built, well-proportioned, moving soundly and carrying himself proudly. Properly clipped in the traditional fashion and carefully groomed, the Poodle has about him an air of distinction and dignity peculiar to himself.

Head and Expression—(*a*) Skull: moderately rounded, with a slight but definite stop. Cheek-bones and muscles flat. Muzzle: long, straight and fine, with slight chiseling under the eyes. Strong without lippiness. The chin definite enough to preclude snipiness. Teeth white, strong and with a scissors bite. Nose sharp with well-defined nostrils. (*b*) Eyes: set far apart, very dark, full of fire and intelligence, oval in appearance. (*c*) Ears: set low and hanging close to the head. The leather should be long, wide and heavily feathered.

Neck and Shoulders—Neck well proportioned, strong and long to admit of the head being carried high and with dignity. Skin snug at throat. The neck should rise from strong muscular shoulders which slope back from their point of angulation at the upper foreleg to the withers.

Body—The chest deep and moderately wide. The ribs well sprung and braced up. The back short, strong and slightly hollowed, the loins short, broad and muscular. (Bitches may be slightly longer in back than dogs.)

Tail—Straight, set on rather high, docked, but of sufficient length to insure a balanced outline. It should be carried up and in a gay manner.

Legs—The forelegs straight from the shoulder, parallel and with bone and muscle in proportion to size of dog. The pasterns should be strong. The hind legs very muscular, stifles well bent and hocks well let down. The thigh should be well developed, muscular and showing width in the region of the stifle to insure strong and graceful action. The four feet should turn neither in nor out.

Feet—Rather small and oval in shape. Toes arched, close and cushioned on thick, hard pads.

Coat—Quality: very profuse, of harsh texture and dense throughout.

Clip—A Poodle may be shown in the "Puppy" Clip or in the traditional "Continental" Clip or the "English Saddle" Clip. A Poodle under a year old may be shown in the "Puppy" Clip with the coat long except the face, feet and base of tail, which should be shaved. Dogs one year old or older must be shown in either the "Continental" Clip or "English Saddle" Clip.

In the "Continental" Clip the hindquarters are shaved with pompons on hips (optional). The face, feet, legs and tail are shaved leaving bracelets on the hind legs, puffs on the forelegs and a pompon at the end of the tail. The rest of the body must be left in full coat.

In the "English Saddle" Clip the hindquarters are covered with a short blanket of hair except for a curved shaved area on the flank and two shaved bands on each hind leg. The face, feet, forelegs and tail are shaved leaving puffs on the forelegs and a pompon at the end of the tail. The rest of the body must be left in full coat.

Color—The coat must be an even and solid color at the skin. In blues, grays, silvers, browns, cafe-au-laits, apricots and creams the coats may show varying shades of the same color. This is frequently present in the somewhat darker feathering of the ears and in the tipping of the ruff. While clear colors are definitely preferred such natural variation in the shading of the coat is not to be considered a fault.

Brown and cafe-au-lait Poodles have liver-colored noses, eye-rims and lips, dark toenails and dark amber eyes. Black, blue, gray, silver, apricot, cream and white Poodles have black noses, eye-rims and lips, black or self-colored toenails and very dark eyes. In the apricots while black is preferred, liver-colored noses, eye-rims and lips, self-colored toenails and amber eyes are permitted but are not desirable.

Gait—A straightforward trot with light springy action. Head and tail carried high. Forelegs and hind legs should move parallel turning neither in nor out. Sound movement is essential.

Size

Standard—The Standard Poodle is over 15 inches at the withers. Any Poodle which is 15 inches or less in height shall be disqualified from competition as a Standard Poodle.

Miniature—The Miniature Poodle is 15 inches or under at the withers, with a minimum height in excess of 10 inches. Any Poodle which is over 15 inches, or 10 inches or less at the withers shall be disqualified from competition as a Miniature Poodle.

Toy—The Toy Poodle is 10 inches or under at the withers. Any Poodle which is more than 10 inches at the withers shall be disqualified from competition as a Toy Poodle.

Scale of Points

	Points
General appearance, carriage and condition	20
Head, ears, eyes, and expression	20
Neck and shoulders	10
Body and tail	15
Legs and feet	15
Coat—color and texture	10
Gait	10
Total	100

Major Faults

Eyes—Round in appearance, protruding, large or very light.

Jaws—Undershot, overshot or wry mouth.

Cowhocks.

Feet—Flat or spread.

Tail—Set low, curled or carried over the back.

Shyness.

Disqualifications

Parti-colors—The coat of a parti-colored dog is not an even solid color at the skin but is variegated in patches of two or more colors. Any type of clip other than those listed in section on coat.

Any size over or under the limits specified in section on size.

bibliography

Arenas, N., and Sammartino, R., "*Le Cycle Sexuel de la Chienne.*" *Etude. Histol. Bull. Histol. Appl. Physiol. et Path.*, 16:299 (1939).

Ash, E. C., *Dogs: Their History and Development*, 2 vols., London, 1927.

Barrows, W. M., *Science of Animal Life.* New York, World Book Co., 1927.

Burns, Marca, 1952. The Genetics of the Dog, Comm. Agri. Bur., Eng. 122 pp.

Castle, W. E., *Genetics and Eugenics*, 4th ed. Cambridge, Mass., Harvard University Press, 1930.

Darwin, C., *The Variation of Animals and Plants Under Domestication*, New York, D. Appleton Co., 1890.

Davenport, C. B., *Heredity in Relation to Eugenics.* New York, Henry Holt & Co., Inc., 1911.

Hart, E. H., "Artificial Insemination." *Your Dog*, March, 1948.

———— "The Judging Situation." *Your Dog*, March, 1948.

———— Doggy Hints. *Men Mg.* Zenith Pub. Co., 1950.

———— "Judgment Day." *Shep. Dog Rev.*, Jan., 1953.

———— *This is the Puppy*, T.F.H. Publications, Inc., 1962.

———— *Budgerigar Handbook*, T.F.H. Publications, Inc., 1960.

———— *This is the Weimaraner*, T.F.H. Publications, Inc., 1965.

———— *The Poodle Handbook*, T.F.H. Publications, Inc., 1966.

———— *This is the Great Dane*, T.F.H. Publications, Inc., 1967.

———— *Dog Breeders' Handbook*, T.F.H. Publications, Inc., 1967.

———— *How to Train Your Dog*, T.F.H. Publications, Inc., 1967.

———— *Enclyopedia of Dog Breeds*, T.F.H. Publications, Inc., 1967.

———— and Goldbecker, *This is the German Shepherd*, T.F.H. Publications, Inc., 1955.

———— Revision, *This is the German Shepherd*—1967.

Keeler, C. E., and Trimble, H. C., "Inheritance of Dewclaws." *J. of Hered.*, 29:145 (1938).

Kelly, G. L., and Whitney, L. F., Prevention of Conception in Bitches by Injections of Estrone. *J. Ga. Med. Assoc.*, 29:7 (1940).

Kraus, C., "*Beitrag zum Prostatakrebs und Kryptorchismus des Hundes.*" *Frankfurter Zeitsch. Path.*, 41:405 (1931).

MacDowell, E. C., "Heredity of Behaviour in Dogs." Dept. of Genetics. *Yearbook*, Carn. Inst.

Moffit, E. B., The Cocker Spaniel, Orange Judd Co., Inc. N.Y., 1935.

Razran, H. S., and Warden, C. J., "The Sensory Capacities of the Dog (Russian Schools)." *Psychol. Bulletin* 26, 1929.

Thorburn, Shooting Directory, 1805.

Stetson, J., "Heartworm Can Be Controlled." *Field and Stream* (June 1954).

Telever, J., 1934. When Is the Heat Period of the Dog?

Whitney, L. F., *The Basis of Breeding.* N. H. Fowler, 1928.

———— *Feeding Our Dogs.* New York, D. van Nostrand Co., Inc., 1949.

———— *Complete Book of Dog Care.* Garden City, L.I., Doubleday & Co., Inc., 1953.

———— and Whitney, G. D., *The Distemper Complex.* Orange, Conn., Practical Science Pub. Co., 1953.

index